The
GALLIPOLI
DIARY

◆

Better Than One

The
GALLIPOLI
DIARY

♦

JONAH
JONES

✳

SEREN BOOKS
*1989

SEREN BOOKS is the book imprint of
Poetry Wales Press Ltd
Andmar House, Tondu Road, Bridgend
Mid Glamorgan

ISBN 1-85411-010-1

Cover lettering: Jonah Jones
Back cover illustration: 'Corris Man' by Jonah Jones

*The publisher acknowledges the financial support of the
Welsh Arts Council*

Typeset in Plantin by Megaron, Cardiff
Printed by Billing & Sons, Worcester

Contents

Illustrations

To Daniel, Robin and William Owain
For God's Sake and the Time Being

"You don't have patience, you don't can working"
(from a broadcast by Andre Certesz, Hungarian photographer)

The Gallipoli Diary

The Eleventh of November, 1969, was not the best of days to climb Cader Idris, but I found myself in a party of eight tackling the ascent on that day. I say 'found myself' because by nature I prefer climbing alone or with one companion only. It was a dark day, with the threat of rain from the west. In a certain strength of wind there is always the chance it will blow off, but on that day it took a long time to make up its mind that it would finally rain us off. At eleven o'clock precisely, as we were still climbing, and well towards the summit, the leader of the group asked us all to stand in silence and remember the dead of two wars. It seemed to me at the time a strange sort of piety, stopping a party on a bleak mountainside to observe the silence of Remembrance Day. Yet it was appropriate. A few of us had been in the war twenty-five years earlier. But still I felt uncomfortable. My father, a First World War veteran, always taught me to forget anything about war, even the remembering on the Eleventh. I don't know why, but that was the way he was. There was a bitterness about his own memory of that war. Normally a jovial man, that was one part of his life he wanted us all to forget.

So we stood, with only the wind in the thin grass breaking the silence of the slopes, and the clouds getting blacker by the minute. We remembered, of course we did, remembered friends who had fallen or been wounded, or even those who had come through unscathed but who had disappeared from our lives in that way that seems unbelievable while you are still in the ranks. And I remembered my father most forcibly, for I had not seen him for many months. His 'little war', he always called it.

We did not climb much farther, we most certainly did not achieve the summit because the weather finally closed in and we had a quick and unpleasant descent. When I got home about three o'clock, my wife was waiting at the door. She looked grave. She said she had bad news for me. "Norman died this morning around eleven", she said. "I couldn't think of a way of getting in touch with you . . . ."

Within the hour I was packed and off by car the two hundred
and fifty miles to pay my last respects to my father.

He left no Will. He did not belong to that stratum of society
that consults a solicitor about property and bequests. He would
have declared, if asked, that he had none. Among a very few
effects he left a number of small pocket diaries. The earliest was
dated 1916. The various items at the beginning of the diary read
oddly now. King George V was 51; carriages with four or more
wheels drawn by two horses required a licence of £2.2s (no
mention of automobiles); a dog licence cost 7s.6d (it is still the
same, i.e. 37½p); letters up to 4oz cost 1d, every additional 2oz
½d. Size limits 2ft by 1ft by 1ft. A licence for a male servant cost
15 shillings.

From time to time I have kept a sort of journal myself, mostly
written in my sketch books if at all. I could not claim to be a
Kilvert or a Pepys, neither in quality, consistency nor scale.
Indeed, I have often thrown bits away, bits written not in book
form but on scraps of paper. I have sometimes regretted this,
because the scrap, in retrospect, has been of more value to me
personally than the sketchbooks. Why I have written thus from
time to time, I do not know, unless I am a compulsive note-taker.
I realise now that I was following an old pattern. Why does one
think something in one's life worth recording? For whom? For
posterity? For one's children, perhaps, that they may see one in a
better light, with judicious editing? For oneself? I would
imagine so, and certainly I have derived on occasion an idea, a
creative line of thought, by browsing through something written
or sketched a few years ago, something that might spark
something off — and artists are forever waiting to be sparked off
by something or other.

Of course, a journal can be embarrassing. For a start it is not
wholly true. There *is* editing by the author, he *is* selective in his
choice of what to record. Unless it be one of those conscientious
diaries that do not last beyond the 31st of January — "Went to
town shopping, had tea at Kardoma, came home tired out and
listened to Beethoven's 6th on the record-player, and so to
bed . . . ". Such a nice life — "tea at Kardoma, Beethoven's 6th
and all that . . . "; leaving aside that the dog had been sick on the
one decent carpet and you and your wife had quarrelled over it
and a precious casserole dish had been smashed during the
washing-up in a fit of suppressed domestic violence in which it
emerged, if truth were known, that it was *you* who had thrown
raw chicken giblets to the poor brute, out of laziness. None of

that is for the well-kept diary.

My father was a compulsive but inconsistent diary-keeper. He nearly always bought a Letts before Christmas, had it put in his stocking by you know who, and piously entered odds and ends in it throughout the year, but with frequent gaps.

I took up that earliest one, 1916, and knew it was not the first. Where, for example, was 1915? He talked so often about friends at Gallipoli, though rarely of any action he took part in. As the 1916 diary opens, the Gallipoli evacuation has just been achieved, one of the 'miracles' of the entire war. It has to be remembered that once the Chiefs of Staff and the Cabinet had decided on that course after the fruitless and costly 1915 campaign. Winston Churchill (*The World Crisis 1911-1918*) talks of bearing losses of 40,000 men in order to evacuate the peninsula. In fact, by some miracle, or by incredible lack of observation from the Turkish lines, the evacuation on the night of December 19th, 1915, was 'achieved' without loss. "The weather," Churchill records, "on which all depended, was favourable for exactly the vital forty-eight hours, and the Turks were utterly unsuspecting. Indeed when dawn broke on empty trenches and famous positions bought at so terrible a cost, now silent as the graves with which they were surrounded, the haggard Turkish soldiers and their undaunted chiefs could hardly believe their eyes".

My father talked of Gallipoli, I recall, with a strange light in his eyes, a sort of fatal fascination. I have the firmest conviction there was a 1915 diary which, if not explicit on military actions, would have indicated his part in the campaign. Even as a child I knew about Suvla Bay. From the way he talked I knew it was a place that had marked him, scarred him for life. Probably it was his baptism of fire; indeed, there can be little doubt of it, for hardly any of the men who charged and occupied those tenuous beachheads, Suvla Bay, Anzac and Helles, were ever out of range of Turkish gunfire. If Australia ever declares itself a republic, the beginnings of that feeling date back to its profound disquiet over the use of its soldiers in the Gallipoli campaign with tragic and, in its opinion, unnecessary and callous losses.

Winston Churchill, as First Lord of the Admiralty, describes the fateful sequence of events with his usual clarity. From the beginning the Dardanelles campaign was vitiated by the historic rivalry of the Naval and Army commands. Lord Kitchener was Secretary of State for War *and* Chief of Staff, so in a way was accountable only to himself in Army affairs, an arrangement much resented by old Lord Fisher, First Sea Lord, who was accountable to Churchill.

It was all, as usual, about Russia. Russia, in relation to the West, assumes the position of being our enemy in peace but our ally in war. The Dardanelles campaign was conceived as an attempt to assist hard-pressed Russia by breaking through the Dardanelles Straits into the Black Sea and thus keeping open a precious supply route. The problem was batteries on either shore and mines in the straits themselves. The choice was either for the Navy, with mine-sweepers, to force an entrance, or for the Army to establish beachheads on the Gallipoli peninsula and to penetrate and destroy as many of these batteries as possible, thus easing the subsequent naval operation. Either way was bound to be costly. Each Chief was jealous and protective of his own Service. Combined Operations seem hardly to have been thought of. However, for political reasons, the Dardanelles campaign was regarded as vital to the total war effort.

In addition, a Dardanelles campaign with its implicit threat to Constantinople was regarded as a means of diverting Turkish attention from an invasion of Egypt, a threat to our communications East of Suez and all that meant to our Empire.

So, 1915 was largely occupied with the campaign and the final evacuation. As my father told the story, that evacuation became a sort of victory, that they had denied the Turks at the very end, when everything might have gone so badly and all be lost. "We crept out like thieves in the night, only our back packs and rifles with us." I would guess the 1915 diary was left behind for some curious Turk to pore over. Nor was the 1916 diary of much help. It was maddening. The year of the Somme, and under September 26th, 1916, all he writes is "Over the top" — just that, yet there they were, climbing over the parapet, often straight into enemy machine-gun fire, flung in in the hope that by sheer force of numbers, sufficient of them would survive to take a few hundred yards of enemy trench and the generals would be able to write in *their* journal (or dispatch, as it was called), that the German lines had been penetrated at such and such a point. As often as not the same few yards were surrendered a week later in the name of 'straightening out a salient'.

But that was the way of my father's diaries. I have to be content with the briefest and most intermittent notes if I am to make any pattern of his life. But so it goes. Like most of the working class, his ancestry is tidied away in the cupboard of social history. There is no tree tracing our family back to the

Conquest or the Reformation. All the males would be in the ranks, the women at the hearth. There is only the Family Bible, a huge tome with brass clasps, which belonged to my paternal grandfather John Jones. In origin John was a Gwent man. I do not recall him ever speaking Welsh and I seem to remember that the last thing he would acknowledge was his Welshness. I find that infinitely sad. Rather would he claim an expertise in pit shafts. He was a shaft-sinker and therefore, like power-station builders today, he was itinerant, moving on as a project was completed. In those days before World War I, the coal industry was expanding and John Jones was doing rather well.

His first move was over the border into Somerset — *Gwlad yr Haf*, Land of Summer — where the small coalfield around Midsomer Norton provided work and a home from home. Here he married Elisabeth Somers. There is a disturbing memory of one of the Somers family in the churchyard at Midsomer Norton. A large stone slab records the tragic death of twelve miners, killed when the cage rope snapped — "it is said, cut maliciously". Were William Somers and his comrades the victims of some Union split?

The first entry in the Family Bible was Llewiza — so spelt, half Welsh, half English. From then on even the half Welsh is abandoned in a rapid succession of names — Phoebe, Henry, Frederick, Charles, Beatrice . . . . In fact the pressures of life and the unfailing fertility of John and Elisabeth soon show in the old volume, for in all Elisabeth bore seventeen children and the Family Bible begins to lapse as a record, rather like Norman's diaries, and my own. After a heady start, John no longer records, whether from a lapse in piety or through sheer domestic forgetfulness I would not know, but remembering his strict Congregational faith, I would guess the latter, for his piety was undiminished to the end.

All this time, John and his ever expanding family were travelling across the country as he exercised his skill and expertise on mine shafts. Eventually they came to rest in Washington in County Durham, where John bought some property, two houses, one of which, Primrose House, I remember well. As for the Welsh connection, that seemed altogether forgotten, though I do remember endless cousins visiting from Somerset; Deightons, Veals, Mills — but never any Joneses. Was John shaking the dust of Wales from his feet? John had family, I know, siblings vaguely referred to, a brother Henry, or Harry. But otherwise all was shrouded in the mists of time, for when I remember John, he was venerable indeed, my father being among the younger members of his family.

As far as I am concerned, my family really begins therefore in Washington, which at the time of John's settling there and in my own infancy, comprised an old village with green, smithy, church and manor house, these days visited by Americans searching for the origins of *their* Washington family. All is now buried in a sprawling New Town quartered by mini-motorways. In those days, neither side so much as acknowledged that there was any American connection. Near the old village but separated by fields, was Washington Colliery, with two pits, the New and the Glebe. John was retired, patriarch of his large family and a pony and trap and a flock of poultry. He tended to keep apart from the generality of his colleagues in the mine, never kept pigeons, nor a whippet, and would never acknowledge that racing existed. His patriarchy was his vocation. His sons gradually married and escaped, his daughters he kept around him as long as possible, like Lear, and when Elisabeth died comparatively young after all that child-bearing, Llewiza (by now Louisa) took over the management of the household and never married. I see her clearly, but recall mostly that she baked the most delicious tea-cakes.

Although retired, John was called on whenever advice was required on the local pit shafts. I remember one occasion when there was an accident and some men were trapped underground and John was called. He was lowered down an old disused shaft and was able to facilitate a rescue. He could judge a risk. It was all in the day's work for John.

I do not remember my grandmother Elisabeth, which was a pity, for by all accounts she was patient, loving and beautiful. My father was sixteenth in succession and Elisabeth was dead before I was three. John I recall vividly. He survived into his eighties on a diet of beef and good baking. He smoked a pipe, but any liquor was anathema. I still have his tobacco jar. It would cost all of £50 to fill it now.

Within the family, old John always used the second person singular. Whether this was from some aboriginal Welsh custom or came from the Somerset argot of Elisabeth I do not know. But John's English I remember distinctly even after all these years. It was slow, Biblical and deep of colour: "Wilt thou come with me, boy?". I expect my eyes were like saucers as I looked up in strict obedience, for to disoblige would have been unthinkable. His beard alone bore similarity to the vision of God that had been passed down to me.

One of my earliest memories is of a ride in the pony and trap. There are parts of Durham that are as verdant as anywhere in the British Isles and in those days the village of West Boldon, clinging to the slopes of the Permian Escarpment, was beautiful, and separated from the conurbation of Tyneside by many green miles. Alas, urban sprawl has now encroached. But on that day, a storm darkened the day as we climbed the hill, and suddenly the sky was rent with thunder and lightning. Before we reached the top the noise was cataclysmic and Sailor the pony was clearly terrified. My grandfather coaxed him towards a barn on the edge of the village and it is still a fresh memory to me — his protective arm round my shoulder, such a rare intimacy from him, while all the time calming Sailor.

I have the impression that all John's sons escaped as soon as they could, either by marriage, by war, or by premature death. Henry died in a pit accident, and another whose name I forgot died at the age of twelve "on his first day in the pit, of an accident". Those surviving all earned good money as coal-hewers, as much as five pounds a week, most of which was dutifully paid into the family coffers. They were then doled out pocket money. My father was a bit of a blade and chafed under the patriarchal yoke. He and his older brother Stanley were often in trouble. My father told the story of a fine summer evening when he and Stanley were playing billiards in Pilkington's Saloon. The upstairs windows were open and cigarette smoke drifted out on to the evening air. (Cigarettes were sinful, pipes were permissible, or is it the usual thing that sons are never allowed what fathers enjoy?) Suddenly John blazed out of Primrose House, stood below Pilkington's windows and shouted for all the village to hear: "Stanley! Norman! Come thee down! Thou art in the midst of Hell!" Shamefacedly they dropped their cues and slunk home to a stern Bible reading from Proverbs: "My son, forget not my law . . . ". Norman could recite that passage by heart for the rest of his life.

It is no wonder that that generation of men marched so willingly to the Kaiser's war. They were so innocent. It was an adventure, and for the working class there had been little enough of that. Charles, Fred, Norman and Stanley were off at once, Norman under age. Charles was killed, leaving a widow who then disappeared, leaving a little granddaughter to add to John's household of daughters. Stanley survived unscathed but Norman sustained a bad head wound at Vimy Ridge in 1917.

After the strict Congregationalist upbringing, Norman must have suffered appalling temptations once he left home. The leaving itself would be traumatic in a family whose normal orbit of travel would not extend beyond what could be atttained by pony and trap or a bicycle. A train journey of any distance was still largely a bourgeois exercise. Holidays were no more than a few days off at home, at Easter to plant the potatoes, in August to have a day at South Shields. The Great War changed all that.

Norman, like most of his generation, was flung at once into the disciplines and temptations of the Army. According to that Letts Diary of 1916 he was Pte Norman Jones (7809), 6th Batt. East Yorks Regt., Mustapha Base Camp, Alexandria, Egypt. His home address is, dutifully, still Primrose House. He was a small, neat man, 5 feet 7 inches in height, eleven stone two pounds in weight, size boots 6. Under the entry 'No. of bank book' and 'Size of gloves' he gives no answer. Neither item had so far graced his life.

On New Year's Day, 1916, despite the Egyptian address, he is on the Island of Lemnos in the Aegean, and the first entry, written very neatly, begins: "Started the New Year in a soldiering fashion. Washed out of camp. We got drownded [*sic*] out in the early hours". The Gallipoli episode is safely behind them and until the next move, they are safe.

January 2nd continues piously enough: "Church in Morning, fine time, 23rd Psalm and Lesson God, Same, Yesterday, Today and For ever. Very Stricking Sermon". As an addendum he notes "Sent letters Home and Mabel".

January 5th reads: "Cemetery Picquet. Searching the Greeks". He was quite prepared to enjoy the natural delights of an Aegean island: "Had a bath in a small stream on Lemnos Island. Sent letter to Mabel".

January 11th indicates a call to arms. He notes iron rations, then: "Left Mudros 7.30 a.m. Embarked and sailed 11 a.m. Landed Imbros 5.15 p.m." As for weather, the Greek Islands are not all they are cracked up to be: "Very wet weather. No more parades". He was not to know he was providing the title of Ford Madox Ford's immortal trilogy. Under January 30th, after reveille at 4 a.m. on a "cold and wintry morning, could not embark Lighter through sea been rough. Slept ready yoked". (He was always a good sleeper in any conditions.) "Sent letter to Mabel".

Next day things improve. "Reveille 2.30 a.m. Left 6.30. Embarked *Ermine* at Imbros for Mudros. Transhipped into

Briton. Slept under table. On Boat guard, got hammocks out. Enjoyed ourselves all day on deck on landing at Alexandria. [February 3] Slept on Deck all night. Sport at night". He is back at base. Cavafy, we may recall, is writing some of his best verse about now, but of that he would not have been aware.

February 4th: "Disembarked *Briton*. Landed at City Beach Camp. Rough night". Alex provided temptation: "Down in Alex with Vincent. Buying silks". For Mabel perhaps? Although later he was to fall, at this stage the old non-conformist piety still prevails. Most of March and April, if sparse on military interest, does record a certain evangelical mood, not uncommon in the First World War, when the preachers got into the camps and conducted their meetings. They were very much part of Empire, searching for souls among our far-flung subjects, but ever ready too, to keep our lads up to scratch. "P.M. Brown converted" Norman records. "Corporal Lilly converted", and so on. Heads were rolling for the evangelists. One imagines the Missions in Alex working overtime, with such an influx of raw material. For death stalked the ranks. The Dardanelles and Flanders were no cushy billet.

Home looms large in the diary, of course. Mabel continues faithfully. Letters to and fro are frequent. Norman bathes regularly in the Suez Canal, once recording difficulties. He was like that, prepared to take risks, to try certain long distances, and to cut corners. Amid all this canal bathing and night duty on signals, a little disillusion seems to set in. "Nothing doing". I remember him as easily bored if there was no action about. But on 16th April they strike camp and by the afternoon they have marched to another bivouac, then on the next day to Ismailia, about midway down the canal.

Oddly enough, I covered much of the same ground myself in the Second World War. I bathed in the Canal with my young wife (just demobilised from the ATS), and in the Great Bitter Lake. We contrived to get lost, deliberately, as only the Army can lose one, so that we should not be separated. It worked, and we weren't. We crossed the Mediterranean like Norman on a troop ship, and altogether the 'Med' voyage was much the same — the last throes of Empire and of our route to the Glorious East and the Jewel in the Crown.

Norman's Eastern Mediterranean tour of duty ends in June 1916 when he embarked at Alex and sailed via Malta for Marseilles. He and his comrades were being mustered for the subsequent slaughter on the Somme. The brief entries thereafter

tell the story of a typical British Tommy in that fateful year.
"Left Ambriends [Amiens?] for Somme district". "Marched up
to Martinsart. Up in the line". He is in and out of the line, the
entries are scribbled in. September 26th reads ominously: "Over
the top". Then: "Bringing in the wounded" — "Mending the
wire at night in the rain".

These brief scribbled entries continue into the New Year of
1917, mixed up in the same diary of 1916. There was neither
time nor opportunity to buy another Letts Diary. Then they
cease abruptly. He was badly wounded in the head at Vimy
Ridge and the rest is silence as far as the diary entries go. He was
returned to Blighty, in a coma.

Besides these brief records of military duty in the worst of
wars, Norman's diaries also record a certain loss of innocence.
Brought up strict Congregationalist, it was in the Army that he
learned both to smoke and to drink. I do not know who Mabel
was, but all references to her cease also. He becomes utterly
independent of home by the end of the war. He has been through
too much to be constrained by Congregational faith, and though
the traditional piety (or was it simply respectability?) remained
with him throughout life, he is no longer, so to speak, card-
carrying. Yet he was keen that his children should have the same
benefits of piety and respect (we were, I now realise, very well
brought-up), but it is left to Grandfather to provide the paternal
rules, to see that we attend Sunday School and learn our verses
for the Anniversary. Norman ended the war a drinking man, and
feeling all the intermittent remorse of a 'back-slider'. On
occasion the drinking got quite heavy and I remember the
bitterness and despair as he mumbled in his cups: "Ah, I'm a
back-slider, a back-slider". The late twenties and thirties had
little to offer a man returned from what he came to call his 'little
war'.

My main impression of him is of a man who never transcended,
and would not altogether wish to transcend, his non-conformist
upbringing.

Despite his Welsh antecedents, he was thoroughly Anglicised,
of that generation for whom Welsh was regarded as some sort of
impediment to getting on in life. Yet, he neither 'got on' nor
maintained his Welshness. His was in many ways the 'lost
generation', lost between two world wars when men forgot roots
and sanity, and trod the eager descent to self-destruction.

Yes, the end of 'Victorian values', the beginning of twentieth
century independence from their constraints. The chief factor

in nineteenth century social relationships was authority, the solidarity of family life and of those religious institutions governing a great deal of that family life. One thinks of Gladstone and his concern over prostitution, of the Band of Hope waging its battle against the demon drink, and of the Salvation Army, with its alternative Command structure. Those boys leaving home for the first time for the Great War marched into it innocent, and shuffled back disillusioned and decimated. They suffered more than should be asked of men however great the peril to the nation. But that was how it was, and when they came back, things were never the same again.

But what of Mabel? Nothing more is heard of her beyond the Gallipoli Diary. After the wounding at Vimy Ridge, Norman is an invalid, hospitalised by his regiment back in East Yorkshire, in fact in Hull, where he met my mother.

My mother Florence was the daughter of a 'sea-going engineer', which always had a romantic ring in my childish ears. She endured one of those Victorian step-mother situations, having lost her own mother early. Florence was in service at a pub with the wonderful name, 'The Marrowbone and Cleaver', in the centre of Hull, next to the market and opposite Holy Trinity Church. She often spoke nostalgically of those days, would tell us war-time stories of Zeppelin raids over Hull, of the bangs and the dust as bombs dropped on the market while she and Topsy, the daughter of the house, clung to each other under the stairs and giggled.

Florence was a tall handsome woman, wearing spectacles — (in late life she was almost blind, and having always been a great reader, she used to boast of her blind book scheme, when people like Sir Laurence Olivier would be reading to her some wonderful classic). She had met Norman while visiting the wounded in hospital in Hull. They were married in Holy Trinity Church, which must have been rather grand, but the war was still on and Norman, head still bound in bandages, was obviously one of its heroes.

I remember his railing at the world later — " 'Homes fit for heroes to live in' . . . ". That idle politician's boast was to haunt Ll.G much as 'Get on your Bike' must surely haunt a present-day pundit. For housing was appalling for the returning heroes. What was it to them that victory in war can render a nation bankrupt?

Oddly enough, it was from my Yorkshire mother that I heard my first Welsh. She was fond of telling stories. I don't think

The family wedding group, 1917. Florence and Norman are seated, centre.

Norman made much of an audience, so we three children would listen rapt as she recalled the halcyon days at the 'Marrowbone and Cleaver'. One tale I remember distinctly was of a 'Norwegian sailor'. "He taught me to count in Norwegian", she would say: "Un, dau, tri, pedwar, pump . . . ", all in passable Welsh, for it was scored in my mind and recalled when later I was to return to the Land of my Fathers. I have often wondered who the monstrous Taffy was, passing himself off romantically as a Norwegian sailor on shore leave.

I was the first of four children. The second, John, died at four months, I suspect of malnutrition during the 1921 coal strike. Nobody wins a war, and the vanquished often pick up the bits quicker than the victors. Certainly, compared with the Edwardian prosperity that preceded the war, the twenty years that followed were dire indeed. This over-riding air of bitterness and frustration affected even us children. The General Strike of 1926 left its mark for life and is still a forcible memory.

Norman had survived his 'little war'; Florence had survived the Zeppelin raids and they had laughed their way to Holy Trinity Church together. The twenties soon knocked the grin off their faces.

I retain one fond memory of my earliest years. I was born at an isolated house called Laverick Hall, a pleasant if austere stone-built Regency-type house out in the country. Our nearest neighbours were the three Browell sisters, who lived in happy Chekhovian squalor in an apple orchard. In the dreadful insanity of those awful post-war years, these three sisters, with their ready giggle, proved a blessing for my poor hard-pressed mother. Even after we left Laverick Hall (I suspect for reasons of non-payment of rent, for the next location was indeed sordid by comparison) my mother would wheel the pram bearing the latest baby the distance to Laverick Hall for a happy gossip with her three friends. They must have provided enormous relief from the grind and deprivation of that time. I have a vague picture of a sort of heaven in my mind, of climbing trees and picking apples in season. Then, back home, to God knows what struggle.

Yes, dire indeed, as anybody from the peripheral areas of Britain in those days will remember. Yet although colliery village life was pretty circumscribed, I was able to satisfy my curiosity about other landscapes. Many people think of colliery landscapes as heavily industrialised wastelands. Yet coalfields is the right name, for places like Durham, Northumberland, the Rhondda and the D.H. Lawrence country of Nottinghamshire were in fact deep country and still are once you get outside the actual villages and towns. In the thirties, movement was still confined to the bicycle at best. Yet this could open whole vistas. Durham Cathedral was the first distant objective (fourteen miles) and the world exploded when first I set eyes on it and entered its vast interior. "The principle of the Gothic architecture", said Coleridge, "is infinity made imaginable". Even then, a callow lad from the drab deprived streets of a colliery village, I saw what he meant without having yet read the words or even knowing who Coleridge was.

My father and I ventured farther. Strapping a tiny bivouac tent to the bicycle we set off over the Pennines and ended up in Borrowdale, in those days practically deserted. We climbed Great Gable, Scafell Pike and the Langdale Pikes and that was the beginning of a long life of hill-walking. Long summer days were spent, mostly in Borrowdale, punctuated only by my father's requirement to sign on the dole.

It was inevitable, then, that I should combine a search for Welsh roots with this love of landscape, especially mountain landscape, by eventually arriving and settling in Gwynedd once I was released from our own 'little war', and had married, far outside the old tribal confines, the girl of my choice. It is all quite a story, like anybody's life. But to be an artist too? It is too much.

And to live where we do?

What a mobile generation we have been, how far we travelled, then slunk back from the outposts of Empire and bedded down, away from the old comfort of the terraces.

Gwynedd Freeman

East of Traeth Bach the hills of Meirionnydd rise steeply, with a roll and pitch above Llyn Tecwyn and on and up to the flat tops of Mynydd Ysgyfarnogod and Clip. It is a lonely stretch with only a narrow strip supporting life, from Harlech to Penrhyndeudraeth. As the ground rises through bracken to bog, rush and sphagnum, even the sheep thin out and a rock-strewn wilderness keeps a walker's pace down. It is a favourite area of mine. Any excuse will serve to take me there. At first the stream beds cut deeply back into a sort of plateau or flat-backed ridge, and the going is hard. But after the first seven or eight hundred feet the flat, broken plateau is reached and a rest is more than welcome. Beyond it the final ridges and folds rise more steeply still, but this long ridge under their shelter has its own separate identity, cut off by bog and stream from the surrounding wilderness and strangely hidden from the sea. This place must once have held importance in the eyes of our early forefathers. Hugging the southern end of this bare, concealed ridge lies the broken detritus of a strange monument. Invisible from the sea and the coastal strip, this monument is nevertheless clearly visible from the tops. Looking down it appears as a delicate circle, like a necklace laid on the flanks of mountain grass. The circular shape is not uncommon — the whole area abounds with circles — but this one is different, more perfect somehow and more delicate in plan. The reason for the relative delicacy is more readily seen as the monument is approached from the Harlech direction, where it suddenly appears against the sky, in profile. It is vaguely like a coronet, though only vaguely because it is made of rough, harsh, granite slabs, natural and undressed, all coruscated by the action of wind and weather. The rocks are long in shape, they point to the sky and, uniquely, they lean outwards, which accounts for the coronet appearance.

It is a wild and solitary place and the only sound, a constant one, is of wind in the grass. Some time, long ago, men foregathered here and worked to a prescribed end — to commemorate and honour some prince or chief. That they chose this place is perhaps not extraordinary. Facing the western sea, these early people must have suffered invasion and pillage, and this place of honour must have represented comparative safety from the depredations of invading mariners. That they chose to build in this deliberate coronet shape is more obscure. Surely it denotes deliberation, design if you like, and that denotes honour for the deceased. What sort of man, or woman, was it that moved men first of all to bear the remains high up into this solitary fastness and then gather quite heavy stones to build his monument in this way? We cannot know. No clue survives and indeed the whole monument by now is almost level with the ground; even the army during the last war dug there. But the original intention or design is still quite patent. We can only surmise. The necrophilic cult that engendered it is not unknown in Wales, and that alone is a feeling shared by that chief's descendants today. Shared too is a common regard for the princely virtues, for however ignorant the Welsh may be of their own ancient history, there nevertheless exists a strong substratum of nostalgia for the days of the rule of the native princes, defenders of the heritage of Wales and patrons of its culture. It may not be explicit, but it is implicit in the way of life, in the attachment to the language, to communal song, to certain institutions sacred and secular and specifically Welsh. And it is implicit in a certain apartness from the English way of life, the equivocal attitude to tourism and the resentment at certain physical intrusions like reservoirs and army artillery ranges.

Bryn Cader Faner, because it exists, because it is surely a monument to a dead chief, is about the most Welsh fact I know. It is among the oldest deposits in that collective unconscious that animates Welshness, embodying locality, pastoral landscape, honour, commemoration and secretive apartness from an alien world. If we but knew the identity of the honoured one, it might be that he confirmed those other elements of the unconscious, the too-ready music, the addiction to alliteration and assonance, rhythm and wordiness, to language and to a slight slyness and craftiness. Bard, politician, priest, whatever he was, he earned his keep, and his funeral. The heights of Ardudwy are a measure of the esteem in which he was held. I am reminded of that sly englyn by W.H. Auden:

> Let us honour if we can the horizontal man
> Though we value none but the vertical one.

Petites Soeurs (1973)

Y Blwyddyn (1971)

But further, not only was there a place of honour in that primordial society; there was room for a designer. In this hard and bare landscape where no malleable material comes readily to hand, there is evidence that men marked and designed things, and the mind that directed Bryn Cader Faner or Bryn Celli Ddu, albeit perhaps a collective mind, had a place in society with the chieftain and the bard and the people. That is evident in the conscious artefacts that have remained of the most ancient and weathered of debris. The designer was another limb of the collective body artistic. Here lies the difference between them and us. For that limb has atrophied and Wales is impoverished for want of precisely its expression.

In Wales landscape predominates, not so much as Dedham informs Constable, or Mont Sainte-Victoire does Cézanne, but rather in its impingement on life. Coal, slate, hill pasture and mountain affect communities mostly strung out in valleys or scattered over hills. History impinges too, for just as Classicism implies an antithetical Romanticism and rarely a synthesis, so the Establishment (and we know what that means) and its implicit radical non-conformist opposition (and we know what that means) have led to a current maladjustment and inwardness in Wales, a sudden inquiry into identity. Hence the internecine dispute over language. The English hardly appear in the argument and do not really understand what the fuss is all about — that is an English prerogative. Of one thing I am sure, that the arts and artists are wrapped up in this identity. Could the Impressionists have been other than French? It is difficult to imagine. They identify France, just as Sibelius identifies Finland. It even works *in absentia* — could Joyce, the life-long expatriate, do anything but identify Ireland? Could Munch the Parisian and Berliner do more than identify the *angst* of his sun-starved birthplace?

So who identifies Wales? My brief is the visual arts and I find little from the past. Richard Wilson was born at Penegoes in Montgomeryshire and buried at Mold, but could he be said to identify Wales? Cader Idris and Snowdon are among his subjects, it is true, but he belonged as much to Rome as to Wales. But this is unfair. Today's issues did not affect his century and when he did paint in Wales he painted like an angel, albeit an Italian one. And in one way Wilson demonstrates an argument, that there have been periods of internationalism in the arts like late Gothic and neo-Classicism which have denied the vitality of native cultures.

It is a matter of accent. Nobody wants to make rules about this. The tide flows constantly, in and out, and internationalism, normally a curative for petty national rivalries and even wars, has flushed life out of too many communities at this late twentieth century stage. Even remote mountain fastnesses like Nepal are now on an international circuit. A return to sources is now required, to attention to the minutiae of landscape, people and living. Internationalism has the tendency to brush aside identity. Against its momentum, individual communities suddenly realise that they are being swept aside, and history has shown what sacrifice they will make, what creative surges they will activate to re-assert that identity. There are signs that Wales is facing the issue right now. Internationalism is remorseless, glacier-like, even logical. It may be too late for Wales as Wales. I believe that the role of the arts in their widest sense will be a major factor in reviving or sustaining what is, after all, a distinctive community. It all means a renewed response to the problems of that distinctness.

My own responses began early in what is now called 'alienation', I suppose. My childhood in the Durham coalfields was not altogether happy. Home was lovely, happy, even through desperate poverty. The years *entre-deux-guerres* offered no more to a Durham miner than to a Rhondda one. But I was an outsider, a loner as a child, without the saving grace of sport to help me out. My father marched from Jarrow to Whitehall, and I got to Jarrow Secondary School and could no more jump over a vaulting horse than over a house. The art room, offering drawing from cubes, cylinders and an occasional dahlia in season, was my only solace. Mostly I remember a sort of melancholy aloofness from the braw life of my companions.

Strangely enough it was the war which helped solve my inner problems. War accented what amounted to rootlessness. Taking my pacifism with me and never carrying a firearm, I marched with others down the old corridors of civilisation, the Mediterranean, France, right into the heart of the Holy Roman Empire. I read David Jones's *In Parenthesis* and was so moved, so impressed by the sheer rootedness of it that I believe it marked a turning-point in my life. Furthermore, its author looked back with pride on the Cockney-Cymro blend of his ancestry and fixed it in this time, this space. Meantime, I well remember, I once looked across the Bristol Channel from Exmoor to the Promised Land and resolved that come what may, I would somehow get to Wales and there root down. *Taid* John Jones had emigrated from the Caerffili area. I would return. Romantic idealism, ill-placed, self-indulgent nonsense perhaps, but listening to the undiluted boyo who ached with *hiraeth* at my side on that height on Exmoor, I felt a great peace and the beginnings of a longing that was a tap-root.

Si la jeunesse savait — and in a way I think it did. Is it arrogance to claim that the pacifism of my youth has been proved right? Of course it is arrogance. And yet the war of 1939-45 seems to have engendered every danger period since. My pacifism was an easy solution — so was Hitler's. Nevertheless, impure as it was, it was the centre of my thinking and feeling about a world in a mess. The stress within one was how to find positive expression, and that, at a time of patriotic fervour, was far from easy. I was not alone. My own ultimate place in war was shared with practically a whole unit, 224 Parachute Field Ambulance, where we put our lives at risk alongside soldiers, yet refused to carry more in the way of arms than a Red Cross armband. I was lost, of course. I knew I wanted to be an artist, that was all, but how to become one was quite beyond me. 'Art' was almost a dirty word in the arid wastes of the unemployment areas that had nurtured me.

I remember having to rush last minute to the training depot at Buxton. Rather earnestly I pushed Burckhardt's *Civilisation of the Renaissance* into my bag, tore an unread story by Dylan Thomas from that week's *Listener* and just caught the train. When I finally settled down that night on a hard bunk, physically and morally uneasy in the unfamiliar khaki, I pulled out the *Listener* page and knew at once why I had torn it out. The illustration was by John Petts, a name unknown to me, but I responded strangely to that drawing. Now what sort of co-incidence was it that made me tear it out of the magazine at such a moment? For next day, finding a kindred soul in that bleak camp and discussing the Dylan story with him and showing him the illustration, he said the same Petts had just left the depot the previous week for parachute training. And so I felt the finger of fate, for it was as dramatic as that for me really. After such a coincidence and in view of my response to the feeling of both story and illustration, I made my formal application for the same parachute course. When it finally got the army rubber-stamp, Petts had left Ringway Parachute School, a fully fledged parachutist. I spent a terrifying month, qualified, and followed Petts to 224 on Salisbury Plain. In a word, Petts was great. I worked with him in the unit. Between operations we pursued our aims. That was how I became an artist, that was the mechanics of it, so to speak. We even had a printing press towards the end and a book, printed in the only available type, 'Verona Roman', on some poor paper scrounged in Jerusalem, describing the medical work achieved by the unit, with rather scholarly appendices on surgery achieved in the field under impossible conditions.

Once demobilised, I worked with Petts at his revived Caseg Press at Llanystumdwy, until I fell ill with pulmonary tuberculosis and he left for a spell at the Arts Council. My illness had been coming, and is still with me, but I have learned to live with it, being now a canny measurer of stamina, reserves, diet, outdoor activity and so on, and I now enjoy enormous good health. Nobody would guess that for five years I endured bilateral artificial pneumothorax (that is, both lungs were mechanically suppressed to about half-cock). The most fascinating text-book on this condition, by the way, is Thomas Mann's *Magic Mountain*.

The measure of all this was to make me a minority man. I was radical though not political. I was so out of step that religion became a defiant gesture in the face of a renascent materialism in western Europe. It infected my work, which was altogether too explicit. I almost became a minor establishment figure in the Catholic Church and found myself working in places like Ratcliffe College and Ampleforth Abbey. I worked outwards from the disciplines of craft. My lettering became quite accomplished but no more. My glass was fair and my sculpture was personal but terribly tentative. While seeking to express a basic philosophy it all seemed to react clean against certain tenets of post-Matisse art that otherwise moved me greatly.

It seemed very late, all told, that I began to mature as an artist. The workshop idea, not the studio, — that was my basic idea. To be like the old blacksmith or the carpenter, to be a member of the community and to be accessible to them, that was what I sought. Of course, I depend on gallery and exhibition sales for part of my income. But if I were wholly dependent on them as an outlet, we should starve, or rather, live on 'social security'. I now depend mainly on work that is commissioned and in Wales it is there. That may be because I am here too, but implicit in that is my workshop attitude; that is, my belief that it is possible to practise Fine Art from the basis of a craft among the people. I would not wish to separate the one from the other, they work together in my mind. The craft in my case happens to be carved lettering, mainly in Welsh Slate, an ideal material. To put it in the simplest terms, to carve letters in slate with a care for their form and disposition is to make a mark. To extending outwards from that mark, to making disinterested marks, is a small step. To shape, saw, construct with and generally manipulate slate is another small step. Disinterested, unapplied work of this sort, manipulation of a beloved material with a basic craft and a searching mind is for me what Fine Art is all about. So the whole work operation is one. I see no precise definition between the respective areas of activity. Nor can I see the place where I work in detachment. It too is part of the whole and inextricable.

Of course, I quite see that this would not do for many of my colleagues and I respect them for what may be greater singleness of mind. Nor could I recommend it as easy. The financial insecurity, the separation from the forum of common-room exchanges at college or school are more than something. I do not say the workshop philosophy will work forever nor do I declare it the definitive solution to Fine Art and identity and their problems. It is quite obvious that in seventeenth century Haarlem, say, painters were as accessible as plumbers and commendable in both cases, (for the Dutch must have smelt better than the rest of Europe, by all accounts) and their painting affirmed an identity that is unmistakable. Why did it not persist then? Well, again it is a matter of accent — a stroll round Frans Hals House soon reveals that painters became *too* accessible. The human race is nothing if not perverse, and has ever been as keen to dismantle as to build, which does not prevent me from regarding Holland today as the nicest of countries to be in.

Nor can the vestigial Welsh part of me be detached from this workshop philosophy. Can these things be measured, anyway? All I know is that Wales matters enormously to me. I am emotional enough to be caught kissing the earth on occasion. If I am absent for more than a day or two, then on my return I must walk my territory and I experience a deep and abiding surge of love in these first few minutes of looking at the estuary which cannot be described. And I recognise people who feel the same as I do in those moments of solitariness and more and more people subscribe to this love, to what has been called a new consciousness. I remember talking to a Porthmadog man and pointing out to him the deep sierra purple colour on the Moelwyns at that moment and he confessed that it never occurred to him to look at the mountains. That I do not understand. Recently I tried to motor from Richmond in Surrey to Islington in north-east London and thought the North Circular would ease my

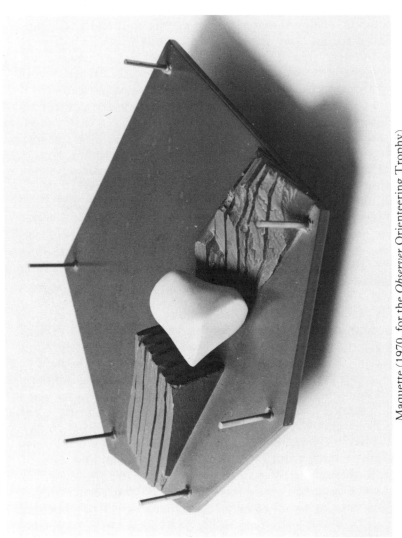

Maquette (1970, for the *Observer* Orienteering Trophy)

problem. After two hours fuming, nose-to-tail, in all the dock traffic I eventually went well past my appointment in time and place and eased out of the traffic and noise into a back street garage for information on where I was in that blasted jungle. I was rather testy, but patiently the mechanic told me. I asked him how he could bear the noise, stink and incessant traffic, all day and every day. "Mate", he said, "I love it". I recognised a kindred soul at once.

Most of my training has been workshop based, and I owe a great debt in particular to Laurence Cribb, whom Eric Gill once described as "one of the angels of this earth". Laurie is dead by now, though it took a cataract on both eyes to prevent him from working right through to eternity. To watch Laurie rhythmically thumping at a block of stone or marble was to watch one of those natural things, like Barry John kicking a ball, or Sobers swinging a cricket bat or Goolagong a tennis racket, a study in absolute economy of rhythm and weight and energy. The stuff would fly off the block and yet Laurie just quietly thumped away with this marvellous stroke that seemed effortless yet got the hammer or mallet on to the chisel head with the maximum weight at the perfect split second and as it did was already bounding back for the next rhythmic thump. It was a good noise to live with and I miss it sorely, for though I have picked it up and must be as good as anybody in the trade these days when not many can actually carve, I know I'll never reach that grace and economy of Laurie's. He has one beautiful inscription in Wales at least, in the old church at Llanfrothen and it was Laurie who taught me to cut letters, and so enabled me to earn a living from the workshop. But he also helped me to establish the workshop ethos, the working through several projects in different kinds, and the working together. For instance, I might be fired by an idea while busy with something else. It was enough to mark out a block and Laurie would start his wonderful pitching, claw and chisel work and we'd work out the idea together — he is wonderful at translating ideas into work. One of my favourites, a horizontal form in white marble which I named 'Leda' was such a project, in which I found my thinking translated by Laurie into the actual marble. The same with the commemorative forms of *Y Tywysogion* group at Aberffraw, much of which was actually carved by Laurie. The old divisions into 'masonry' and 'sculpture' were cancelled out by people like Laurie and his master Gill, and I am happy to continue the tradition. There seems a fear in Britain that carving denotes a rather meretricious

kind of traditional art, mostly figurative in a boring way. There
is reason for this, for a great deal of academic work in stone has
killed what was once a noble expressive art. And the 'direct
carving' advocated by Moore, Hepworth and Epstein seemed to
go down one avenue only. My own choice of pedigree would be
to return to the first source in this century, Brancusi, and look
at other channels than these sculptors. Isamu Noguchi the
American-Japanese is such an example. Noguchi's workshop
practice, his manipulation of stone and marble, his capacity to
treat whole environmental projects as sculpture, like transforming
a hillside near Jerusalem into a most exciting outdoor museum or
the gardens of the United Nations building at Paris into a
thrilling complex of shape, texture, water and tree and natural
materials, this is what it is all about.

Brancusi furthermore is a great exemplar in life style. For me
he is the most complete man this century has produced. He, and
his work, have an implosive quality that contrasts strangely with
the divisive alienation of modern society. Students turn to Zen
or follow a guru — Brancusi was his own complete quiet centre
in a phrenetic world. He did not forget sources either — there is
myth from Roumania externalised in his work which transcends
time and fashion. And always, throughout his life, he simply got
on with it, and allowed others to do the debating. He would have
walked with me to Bryn Cader Faner, I'm sure he would, and he
would have taken in its inherent myth in its native landscape and
he would have come away and later, perhaps years later, he
would have translated the experience into some abiding form
that belonged to our own time and yet would transcend all time,
would transmit its own myth and yet display a kinship with that
old myth that once animated these hills. Brancusi got away from
the object — he put things up that hinted at scale and space, and
this at a time when the object was supreme. Brancusi imparted a
timeless, infinite, unconfined quality to even the smallest object
and is my own touchstone in the current debate on the validity of
the art object. This argument, of the object, as against its
concept, is a non-argument once you withdraw art from its false
luxury status. Brancusi was a workshop man who never liked art
on an exclusive pedestal. I believe artists are disturbed by the
destination of art as a sort of super currency, and rightly so.
What validity is there in Van Gogh selling one canvas in his
lifetime for four hundred francs, and then the whole corpus of
his work being beyond price not fifty years after his death? But
once art is common-place, the product of workshop activity,

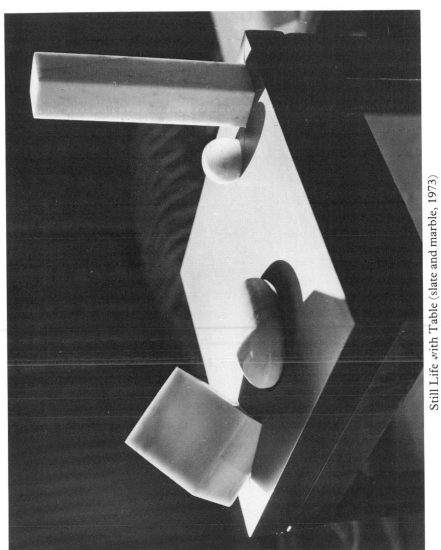

Still Life with Table (slate and marble, 1973)

something from the back streets of Haarlem, Florence or Paris, then the object is as undebatable as Zbigniew Herbert's *Pebble*:

> . . . equal to itself
> mindful of its limits
> filled exactly
> with a pebbly meaning . . .

And looking at Brancusi, or even Noguchi his pupil, I see an affinity with those early builders of Bryn Cader Faner, a concern not only with the object but with the environment, with landscape and its myth, with time present, past and future. I would like to think that I left behind me in Wales a thing or two of which the same could be said. But I am also aware that it's a tall order and the greatest dimension of all, Time, seems the shortest.

The Magic Mountain?

Medicine has taken a beating lately. Over-use, even abuse of drug prescriptions, ignorance of side effects, confusion over priorities, decline of the bedside manner: all these have tarnished the Dr Finlay image. Nobody seems to know whether the National Health Service is being cut or being expanded. It has become a minefield of political polemic. Pleas for various fringe practices like homoeopathy, hypnosis, acupuncture and faith-healing have added to the present uncertainty in a field once unquestioned.

To the majority of the population, there has not been a time when the National Health Service did not exist. Only those born before the forties can claim experience of pre-NHS medicine. I remember distinctly those prehistoric days, when the working class paid for medicine by subscribing to a sixpence or shilling-a-week 'club'. Very few enlightened employers arranged schemes for their workers and families. By and large, only the well-off could claim the commanding heights of medicine, in the sense of getting the right treatment when, how and where they wished, without waiting on some long queue. The rest depended on what was called 'The Panel' — (why, I've never known, unless it referred to the panel of doctors, since doctors seem to congeal into 'panels'). Our particular Panel doctor bore the Happy Family name of Dr Stitch, which did not help when he picked up a pair of gleaming tongs and opened your nostrils for scrutiny of your adenoids, which, along with tonsils, seemed to be the staple of child medicine.

Only that generation can view progress from actual experience. Perhaps the greatest measure is in the once great scourge of tuberculosis. In the colliery village where I was reared among rows of bleak, identical terraces, every so often there would be a house which had its upstairs windows completely removed. Inside would lie some wretched victim, open to all weathers, taking the prevailing treatment for most terminal cases. Antibiotics had not yet been discovered, of course, and only a small percentage of cases were considered worth hospitalisation. Again, the wealthy had resort to special treatment, mostly in Switzerland or on the Côte d'Azur. The particular society they engendered is the source of inspiration for Thomas Mann's great dialectical masterpiece *The Magic Mountain,* where febrile argument between rational and scholastic schools is aired against a background of rarified romantic intrigue and off-stage medical treatment. The cynosure in all this is the attractive Madame Chauchat, whom I always visualised as a delicate version of Marlene Dietrich. I suspect the real seat of her 'illness' might have been found in Monsieur Chauchat, who does not appear in the book, and who is obviously relegated to 'the plains' as beneath consideration.

For most, however, the Magic Mountain was beyond reach, and a network of local sanatoria existed for more ordinary mortals. Charitable foundations like the King Edward VII Memorial scheme in Wales kept these establishments going, and were eventually subsumed into the NHS. I am one of a small band who by accident can claim experience of both the Magic Mountain and the local sanatorium.

In the last war, I was attached as a medic to the 1st Canadian Parachute Battalion. During the great sweep across France, Belgium, Holland and Germany, we liberated quite a number of labour camps, not to mention the actual nadir, Bergen-Belsen. Since our own casualties were sometimes light in the general sweep, the medics' main concern was often with trying to help those victims of the camps. There was chaos everywhere, the prisoners often wandered aimlessly about (Primo Levi's book *If not now, when?* is revealing on this episode in Europe's agony). Malnutrition, chronic disease, and not least, tuberculosis, were widespread. Antibiotics were just coming in. I believe I first contracted the disease then, for despite my lowly upbringing, I had always enjoyed robust health, mainly due to my mother's acute deployment of resources. Over-feeding can be sometimes more harmful, and there was no fear of that in the thirties. Certainly the Airborne Forces found no reason to reject me when I sought to volunteer. But Europe was starving and could be said to be running with disease. I took a long time to succumb. It was two years later that a developing cough refused to go away and I made a rare visit to the family doctor. He declared I was 'over-doing it', I should put my feet up and relax. Six weeks later I was worse and he packed me off at once to a specialist under the new National Health Service. In less than a week I was in one of those inherited King Edward sanatoria, at Llangefni in Anglesey, receiving the very best treatment. Before the war, I should have died young in one of those windowless rooms. Like Keats, Chopin, D.H.Lawrence, Katherine Mansfield or Llewelyn Powys, I should have been denied the years of maturity watching our children growing up and they in turn developing.

The Romantic obsession with death implicit in so much of Keats was inevitable. "Why did I laugh tonight?" he writes in one of his best-known sonnets, and you can feel him railing against fate. "Darkness! ever must I moan, To question Heaven and Hell and Heart in vain". When you are feverish with this wasting disease, nights are indeed melancholy.

> Yet would I on this very midnight cease,
> And the world's gaudy ensigns see in shreds;
> Verse, Fame, and Beauty are intense indeed,
> But Death intenser — Death is Life's high meed.

Tuberculosis was the great scourge of genius and nonentity alike. I was fortunate. With a three centimetre cavity on one lung and 'fluffy infiltration' on the other, I might have been doomed. But I benefitted from both the NHS and the new drugs. I still had to endure the traditional mechanistic treatment of artificial pneumothorax, that is, the partial deflation of both lungs by introducing air between the lungs and their supporting rib-cage. Each week I had to submit to a thick hollow needle, which the surgeon pushed between ribs. He (and later she) then allowed measured amounts of air to flow in. At first, to enable this delicate air balance to settle down, I had to lie prone, then after a few months I was allowed to sit up and then gradually to find my feet.

I was far from alone, of course. Many Welsh men and women of advancing years will recall similar experiences. Indeed, in Welsh, the illness bears dread connotations — *darfodedigaeth* — literally 'fading away'.

After twelve months to the day, I was released and returned to the bosom of my family, then I was sent by the Airborne Forces Security Fund to a large hospice devoted entirely to Parachutist and Commando Lung cases, in Leysin, five thousand feet up in the Bernese Oberland. The village then was given over completely to the treatment of tuberculosis, a Magic Mountain similar to Davoz-Platz. Hans Castorp sets the tone in Thomas Mann's masterpiece: "Here, after a long and windy wait in a spot devoid of charm, you mount a narrow-gauge train; and as the small but very powerful engine gets under way, there begins the thrilling part of the journey, a steep and steady climb that seems never to come to an end". With both lungs suppressed, I had difficulty in breathing and moving. For five months through an Alpine winter I walked about slowly on a stick and was very thin. But it helped. The medicos knew what they were doing. When I returned to the plains I found by contrast that I could breathe with ease, and with the expert guidance of the Rehabilitation Officer I soon recommenced work as free-lance artist. I still had to endure bilateral pneumothorax for five long years, each week returning to the clinic for those painful needles.

It is a measure of both the NHS and of medical progress that now, thirty-five years on, hardly any of this exists. Leysin is a ski resort. TB Sanatoria are practically non-existent, the old mechanistic and surgical treatments have given way almost completely to drug medication. And of course, improved social and housing conditions have reduced the incidence of TB drastically. That wide-open window in the colliery or quarry terrace where little Nell lay dying is a thing of the past, provided we cherish the achievements of the last forty years. So I view the NHS and medical progress with immense gratitude. From death's door I have enjoyed vigorous health, enabling me to practise 'my craft and sullen art'.

I can pass on a few holistic tips, of course, for part of the fight must come from within oneself. First, work is the best therapy, if you can manage it, and that is why, wherever we can achieve it, we must bring the disabled into our normal working lives and not leave them outside in the cold. Next, a good diet is essential, good food that is to be enjoyed, not just 'fad' food. For my part, a long daily walk is vital. I don't stroll — I really go at it, for we live on humpy ground on the edge of Yr Wyddfa. Above all an enjoyment of life is both a means and an end in good health.

And I have an idea that, as old age approaches, the same regime will apply, for once again, as with the disabled, we tend to exclude the old when we might sometimes bring them in more. I know of one lady friend, aged eighty-plus, who enjoys her walks and does not stint them. Not only her figure retains its youth but her attitude to life is enhanced by a sharp-eyed awareness.

And there are countless things to avoid. I shall not enumerate them, even if I were certain I knew what they were, but I will leave the last word of warning with Thomas Mann as he bids farewell to his hero Hans Castorp and his generation:

They were roused in the night, brought up in trains to morning, then marched in the rain on wretched roads — or no roads at all, for the roads were blocked, and they went over moor and ploughland with full kit for seven hours, their coats sodden. It was no pleasure excursion.

Hans was to be one of those who marched to that war which engulfed our fathers or grandfathers. Yes, that fate we must avoid — or all the medical and other social progress we have made will be for nothing.

Y Dinas Anweledig
(The Invisible City)

After the generations of dispersion of the Welsh diaspora, the accidents and upheaval of war at least brought the blessing of my own return to Wales. In those days after the war, it was quite evident to the newcomer in Wales that the old language was dearly loved, and in Eifionydd, where we first lived, it was the dominant language. Nevertheless, certain compulsions to speak the language did not then exist as they do now. In the press of earning a living as an artist, of practically building a house, and in the daily compulsions of creative art, I found little enough time to learn Welsh (I remember the sheer fatigue of living and working, and if anybody had suggested evening classes I doubt if I could have lifted a finger). And as I say, nobody bothered about Welsh, even if everybody spoke it. It was later, when the movement towards the single issue of the Welsh language gelled into action of various kinds, and when the Welsh speakers realised their language was indeed under threat and could die for want of support against the daily inroads of the English-speaking media, that the compulsion to learn and speak Welsh became apparent. In post-war days, all Council minutes were in English, you could not register the birth of your child in Welsh, you could not swear an oath in court in Welsh nor plead your case, and all official forms from rate demands to medical prescriptions were in English. All road signs were in English only, no government department recognised Welsh (one of our children always points with pride at the *Post Brenhinol* on the Post office vans, having landed in jail at one time for smashing a wind-screen or two). Despite a clear disability to learn a language, I wish the present compulsions had been there when finally the Army released me to Wales, for I might have had more Welsh than I have now. I do feel deprivation, and I do applaud the resuscitation of Welsh, the renewed pride in its survival and use. That hoary chestnut that it 'holds you back' was ever a nonsense, for all our children are bi-lingual and have achieved a high success in life and in work that requires literacy and flexibility of mind. That is a matter of pride for my wife and me — but it does not give me enough Welsh to get by — and that is a matter of sorrow to me.

British society is not made up of classes, Huw Wheldon once claimed, so much as *clubs*, and Welsh speaking was one of the great clubs of which he was proud to be a member. I knew what he meant, but not being a club man myself I preferred another image. I have always been attracted by the concept of the 'city' — not that great collection of civic buildings and sprawling suburbs that we usually mean — but rather that community of souls implicit in St Augustine's *De Civitate Dei*, or those imagined in Calvino's *Le Citta Invisibili*. Yet by nature I am either a nomad or a rustic and belong to no city, whereas Huw belonged very much. I long to belong, but in the end resist, or find myself incapable of learning the city's precepts or of accepting its laws. It all amounts to a refusal to belong and I have come to live by that. But if I spoke Welsh fluently, I would belong, at last, to a 'city' and I would be proud and grateful, and revel in its institutions. For there is a city of Welshness in that abstract sense which conjoins all Welsh-speaking men and women. Once a year it foregathers at its appointed caravanserai and then disperses to the four winds. As a 'city', *yr Eisteddfod Genedlaethol* (the National Eisteddfod) would qualify admirably for yet another of Calvino's invisible cities:

> This city which cannot be expunged from the mind is like an armature, a honeycomb in whose cells each of us can place the things he wants to remember: names of famous men, virtues, numbers, vegetable and mineral classifications, dates of battles, constellations, parts of speech . . .

But I never quite arrive at the city. My mind refuses to enter the honeycomb so that not belonging is my constant state. Simply put, I have never got beyond a feeble reading of Welsh because I am unable to travel the distance. Implicit in that statement, of course, is an admission that I am travelling *from* somewhere. I have been travelling since I was very young, from the assumptions of empire that the speaking of English still implies. There have been two great imperial languages, Latin and English, and each has moved like a great glacier across the face of the earth, carrying and burying all before it. Celtic tongues from Asia Minor to Achill Island have succumbed over two millenia, with a few terminal moraines like Welsh and

Breton remaining, still suffering erosion by the remorseless glacier of the universal tongue.

Awareness of Wales and the Welsh language and Welshness is not easily accessible to those beyond Offa's Dyke. Welshness is quite secretive, keeping itself to itself.

When, after demobilisation, my wife and I finally cut loose and left family, roots and jobs to live in Wales, I remember the culture shock as we entered Gwynedd by train for the first time. At Conwy station, we opened the window to hear a newsboy shouting *"Cymro!"*. I had not known. A Welsh weekly existed and was being sold on the street. It is sad, probably, that no newsboy would be seen these days selling *Y Cymro* on Conwy station. The frontier has moved back. And yet Welshness persists, praise God and a certain stubbornness. It is wrapped up in the Welsh language and the daily, colloquial speaking of it.

I know that if I spoke Welsh with fluency, I would *be* different, a citizen at last. I would slough the inherent assumptions of Roman, Holy Roman, British and American imperialism and would belong to what Theodor Roszak called the Counter Culture. I would speak the language of my fathers, of a people whose language has not spread over the earth and has not required others to speak it in order to succeed in the affairs of state.

It is the very strength of this persistent, remote city which attracts me. For empires fade, even as we see in our own time the retreat of the great American dream from all the corners of the world. Is it that polo, whisky pegs, Singer's sewing machines and Coca-Cola are not enough to erode what is native and natural? For Welshness is one of those abiding 'cities' whose ethos persists against the spread. That persistence is not a mere political posture. I would regard the statistic of one-hundred-thousand readers of *papurau bro* (local Welsh language newspaper) as of more significance than seats in Westminster. Political posturing is an imperial assumption, that politics propose and dispose. But the surviving 'cities' do not propose and dispose: they merely persist, and in the simple persistence lies "the honeycomb in whose cells each of us can place the things he wants to remember". For Welshness consists of that long memory, of that long persistence against the glacier, of speaking, reading, writing, broadcasting, dreaming, loving and playing in a language whose character denotes a special 'city'.

If I had the capacity to travel that remaining distance, and could speak that language instead of lamely reading it like a foreigner, then I would enter the city and would take off my travel-stained sandals and be glad to be at last within the city walls. As it is, we have sent our children on as able ambassadors.

It is often the position of the artist to be an outsider. Perhaps it is a necessary state to certain artists, or perhaps they are artists because of it. But every outsider is travelling from one place to another. The most notorious was Gauguin, of course, who left his money-changing city to embrace a 'city' of Polynesia. Sometimes, as with Cézanne, the journey is more interior. David Jones lived the greater part of his life in London, but travelled daily inwardly towards the city of Welshness, without ever entering. These are great exemplars, explorers, but that is how I feel, travelling sometimes in their steps, seeking a city but never reaching it. And I thought I did not mind, so long as the city remained and I was welcome to live under, if not within its walls.

And yet I realise I *do* mind. My inability to learn the language is like a terminal illness. It might have been diagnosed earlier and arrested while there was still hope. Now, alas, it is far too late. I curse my sheer intellectual incapacity to learn and retain Welsh. Do I blame myself too much? It may be. I am a poor learner of anything requiring memory. I am as incapable of learning needing memory (like music, poetry, or learning a language, any language) as some people are incapable of drawing a decent representation of something. Some part of my poor brain functions to the exclusion of another. What is one to do? I have words like *etifeddiaeth* (inheritance) scored in my funny head from the beginning yet forget the simplest vocabulary or sentence construction as soon as I have learned it. It is one thing painfully to read Welsh with the aid of *y geiriadur*, quite another to comprehend and respond to the speech of the 'man on the street'. It saddens me, this inability. It has meant a closed door. I have never been able to enter that city of Welshness which depends for its sustenance and survival on its native Welsh language. I am virtually apolitical. Politics and the ways and means of politics do not move me much, yet I feel deeply that the Welsh language is a political issue, in the sense that *polis* means city, and the destiny of the Welsh people, including the English-speaking majority, their identity, their distinctness, their individual problems and solutions is inextricably wrapped up with the native language. Any monoglot English-speaking Welshman or English immigrant to Wales who denies this seems to me fundamentally wrong *and* wrong-headed.

And yet, feeling all this very strongly, *knowing* the sheer logic

Etifeddiaeth (white Ancaster stone, 1987)

of it, I still cannot learn Welsh. I have tried, but then the door closes. Why? Well, firstly it has to be said that Welsh *is* a very difficult language to learn. Here I have found some Welsh people rather unforgiving. They imply that nothing is easier than learning Welsh, that if they can switch to English where necessary, then surely an English-speaker can soon become bilingual the other way. But not so. I have used the image of a glacier to describe the effect of the universality of English. It is the Latin of modern times, and even the proud French seem to succumb these days. Secondly, Welsh, as one of the oldest tongues, has the strangest structures to a learner. Thirdly, there are inherent divisions within Welsh itself, the disagreements among even academic Welshmen as to what is good Welsh. There is a disparity between written and spoken Welsh that to a learner is more than a passing impediment. It is almost as though they were two different tongues. I can understand this. It is as though a Frenchman tried to learn English from the language spoken in the street. I often have to ask a Cockney to repeat a sentence, his English is so far removed from my own. The Geordie that prevailed where I was born would be quite inaccessible to an outsider. "Ah'm ganna gan yem the neet and nowt's ganna stop us" must be translated as "I'm going home tonight and nothing is going to stop me".

In my carving *Etifeddiaeth*, commissioned by Cyngor Dosbarth Dwyfor, I depict three generations, and in handing it over ceremoniously to the Chairman of the Council I said "*Gobeithiaf fod y Neges yn ddigon clir*" (I hope the message is clear enough). And I really meant it, for what the carving is saying, I hope, is that a heritage, a language, is passed down mainly by the female line — that it is no wonder we call it the *mother-tongue*, never the father-tongue. And so long as the women of Wales have a care for the language and for passing it on, then it will persist and flourish. "In youth is pleasure", said Shakespeare, and he might have said the same for learning too, for past a certain age, those things requiring memory for learning are beyond some of us. That, at least, is my own experience. The city will be for ever beyond my reach — but that does not for one minute diminish my belief in it, my need for it, and my deepest love for it. It is a matter of pride that, after the generations *di-Gymraeg* (without Welsh), I now hear daughter and grandson conversing again in the old tongue.

Portraits

There is a particular spur of the Moelwyn range of mountains in Gwynedd which finally falls into the sea as the narrow peninsula known as Trwyn Penrhyn, or Aber Iâ, and now mostly as Portmeirion. On either side of this peninsula lie the estuaries Traeth Mawr, which carries the river Glaslyn to the sea, and Traeth Bach, which carries the Dwyryd. It is an area which for some reason has attracted more than its fair share of eccentrics. The nearby township of Porthmadog owes its existence to Williams Maddocks, Member of Parliament for Boston in Lincolnshire in Napoleonic times. It was he who, coming from an area of dykes and polders, thought of damming the Glaslyn estuary, thus creating a vast tract of grazing land behind the 'Cob', and incidentally easing transport from the east towards his projected port for the Irish Packet-boat on the Lleyn peninsula. This latter never came about, for Holyhead was eventually chosen, leaving Maddock's new town of Tremadog and the nascent Porthmadog high and dry.

Percy Bysshe Shelley visited Maddocks at his house, Tan-yr-Allt in Tremadog, there completed his poem 'Queen Mab', and caused a certain amount of local consternation by putting maggotty sheep out of their misery, thus raising the ire of local farmers, who have their own recipes for dealing with the multifarious diseases of sheep.

Still the area attracts its eccentrics. Clough Williams-Ellis the architect and his wife Amabel the writer lived at Plas Brondanw on the lower slopes of Moelwyn Mawr. John Cowper Powys lived out his last years at Blaenau Ffestiniog within sight of the mountain. Bertrand Russell settled for his last years in Plas Penrhyn, a small mansion overlooking Traeth Mawr. Arthur Koestler lived here a while, and on the eastern shore of Traeth Bach, Richard Hughes the novelist lived the greater part of his life and died there. And so on.

Is it the climate? It may be. The area knows little frost and enjoys its own special micro-climate, though rain can be plentiful in a wet season. On the other hand, in a good season it is absolute heaven, with the blue of the mountains framing the golden sands of the estuary and shore. Is it the comparative isolation from the rest of Wales and more particularly from England? It may be, for although the isolation is easily felt and probably enjoyed by those who settle here, it takes a not too arduous journey to get out and to London if need be. It is even possible to travel all the way from Porthmadog and Penrhyn-deudraeth to Euston by train, and though I recommend the glorious scenery all the way to Shrewsbury, it is not the quickest way to London if time be of the essence. Is it the very air, which inspires creativity? It very well may be. Whatever, it is still an odd and closely knit community, eccentric or not, and my wife and I have enjoyed it immensely since 1948 when our generation began to settle after our own war, to rear a family and carve out our lives in the peace that is possible in this landscape.

Bertrand Russell (1968)

Bertrand Russell

Although we lived very near to Bertrand Russell at his last home on the same estate, we did not press our neighbourliness. He had several devoted friends in the area, notably Clough Williams-Ellis, Michael Burn the writer, Sir Osmond Williams our amiable peninsular landlord, and Rupert Crawshay-Williams the philosopher, whose book affectionately chronicled Russell's last years at Plas Penrhyn. However, Clough asked me to carve a profile of the great man, and rather diffidently I sought a meeting to arrange sittings.

As soon as I saw Bertie (as we all called him with the presumptuous lèse majesté of mere neighbours), I knew a polite profile was not the right answer. So I asked him if I might make a full portrait bust of him and he readily consented on condition it did not take too much of his time. There was already a bust of him by Epstein, which stood on a plinth in the hall. Epstein is probably the greatest modern portrait sculptor after Rodin, but his head of Bertie is heavy, devoid of the impishness that characterises him. I felt no particular compunction about following the master. I promised myself no more than three sittings of an hour each. It meant carrying my tripod and clay in and out of the house each session which is hard work, but it seemed a unique opportunity. Russell was slumped comfortably in his library chair, with a book and a pipe always at hand should I prove too insufferable. He was tiny, like a small bird, very much alive and alert. It was a family trait, for the first Earl, Lord John Russell, had been so small that he had been nurtured like a tender plant even though he survived to a ripe old age. Bertie asked me if he might talk and I said I would prefer him not to pose, but rather do as he pleased, talk or read, above all not feel obliged to entertain me, for he was unfailingly gracious in his social manners. So he talked. Although I was then all of forty, he treated me rather as a young spark. We discussed English literature, he a little *de haut en bas*, I undergraduate at a tutorial. I remember the warmth in his voice as we got round to his old friend Joseph Conrad. We came to one particular novel I had lately read and which I regarded, I said, as best after *Nostromo*. He wanted to know which one, but preoccupied as I was I reeled off in the woolliest manner a rough description of the chief character and various episodes in the novel. I could not for the life of me remember the name of the character or the title of the novel itself. At once Russell interjected: "You no doubt mean Flora de Barral in *Chance*" The rapidity of his total recall, the way facts and names came forth immediately as though from a computer, made me realise how woolly and second-rate my mind was in the face of his first-class one.

Yet I remember most vividly that at the last sitting he asked me which other English novelist of this century had impressed my 'young' mind and when I replied "Lawrence" he became quite irrational in his distaste for that old friend and enemy. "Ran round the kitchen after his wife with a carving knife. Quite an uncivilised monster, Lawrence, *not* a great writer!" It was no use arguing, for he may be right. It depends where you stand. Surely if ever a man lived by "the holiness of the heart's affections" it was Lawrence, but it was not a criterion that would have convinced Bertie. Myself, regardless of Lawrence's personal character, I would place *Women in Love* among the best dozen novels of the century. I suspected a bitterness of experience in Bertie's view of Lawrence. It was rather like asking for an opinion of Beethoven from that long-suffering nephew of his. However, a little research rather confirmed the lapse into violence, and the latest biography of Katherine Mansfield, by Claire Tomalin, not only confirms the story, but suggests too that Katherine may have contracted tuberculosis from Lawrence. There is no way of checking such things by now, though I do recall the passion with which Bertie denounced Lawrence and this was, so to speak, a living contact.

Bertie's family had a history of eccentricity, and certainly one of kicking over the traces. His parents Lord and Lady Amberley were much abused in their time for their championship of Malthusianism and the sexual emancipation of women and any amount of liberal causes calculated to infuriate stuffy Victorian society. Then, when they died young, Bertie was left in the care of his grandparents at Pembroke Lodge in Richmond Park.

> The grown-up conversation to which I listened was mostly of things that had happened long ago; how my grandfather had visited Napoleon in Elba, how my grandmother's great-uncle had defended

Gibraltar during the American War of Independence . . . . I should be told how Carlyle had called Herbert Spencer a 'perfect vacuum', or how Darwin had felt it a great honour to be visited by Mr Gladstone. (*Autobiography*)

The early death of his parents certainly affected his attitude towards life. "I owe to the Russells shyness, sensitiveness and metaphysics, to the Stanleys vigour, good health, and good spirits. On the whole, the latter seems a better inheritance than the former".

He succeeded to the title when his elder brother was stripped of it upon being tried and found guilty of bigamy by his peers. His family seems never far from scandal, for either their opinions or their conduct. His successor to the title had the doubtful honour of being thrown out of the House of Lords for a speech which in its condemnation of police behaviour went far beyond the bounds of the permissible. Bertie's uncle Lord Stanley of Alderley converted to Islam in the latter half of the last century and married the same lady four times, twice by the Mohammedan rite and once by the Roman Catholic one. All were equally invalid since the lady had another husband still living. Lord Stanley restored the church at Llanbadrig in Anglesey to look like a mosque. Since Llanbadrig is reputedly one of the spots where St Patrick set off to convert the Irish, there seems a double sacrilege about this.

Bertie would relate that he had held the hand that had shaken the hand of Napoleon, which was true of course, because of that meeting of his grandfather and Napoleon on Elba. It was one of many odd little facts that Bertie bestowed upon one when meeting him, that one had shaken the hand that had shaken the hand that had shaken that of Napoleon. This apostolic pressing of the flesh was the sort of small talk that could always arise in Bertie's company. It was much more likely than some Platonic dictum. Rather it might be some argument turned on its head by ridicule. "I can't think why people accuse me of being anti-American. After all, fifty per cent of my wives have been American".

Am I right in supposing he will be remembered as philosopher, mathematician and rebel with too many causes, while it is generally forgotten that he was awarded the Nobel Prize for Literature? He delighted in *that* story, for when he was flown over to receive the prize he balked at the plane, protesting he would *die* if he wasn't allowed to smoke his pipe. The stewardess, defeated, eventually allotted him a seat at the rear of the plane. The plane crashed into a fjord, twenty-five passengers died and Bertie was among the few survivors plucked out of the water. Asked how he felt as he was about to meet his Maker he replied: "I felt the water was bloody cold". He would go on to claim that it was demonstrable that tobacco saved life, because had he not insisted on having his pipe during the flight, he might have sat farther down the plane and gone down with the rest of the passengers. The prize was fully deserved, for his three-volume *Autobiography* and his *History of Western Philosophy* alone earn it. His prose is lucid and rings of an awful honesty. How many men, for instance, would admit that a love affair, such as his with Lady Ottoline Morrell, described with such rhapsody, could fade because he developed acute halitosis due to bad teeth?

Like many Victorians he was an indefatigable letter-writer. His archives, which the nation has allowed to be sold abroad, contain no less than 25,000 letters. There is still, in my opinion, no better way of distant communication and I wish the telephone had never been invented by that other Victorian. Imagine the loss to literature had Byron had access to the telephone. His letters, all twelve volumes, are among the most revealing documents of a vivid life and times.

In 1963, when the world waited with baited breath for the outcome of the Cuban crisis as President John F. Kennedy and Communist Party Secretary Nikita Khruschev squared up to one another and the use of atomic weapons was not beyond the realms of possibility, Bertie played a crucial part in bringing the two global gladiators to a point when they might talk sanely rather than hurl insults at one another. At that time I employed a local slate mason who was desperate for work when the Porthmadog Slate Works closed down. He had such a large family that he supplemented his wages by moonlighting as a telephonist on night-shift at the local exchange. It was not, I gathered, an arduous duty and most nights he could sleep by the switchboard undisturbed by callers after midnight. But during the Cuban crisis he turned up for work looking very much the worse for wear and by mid-morning had committed what was unthinkable for such a skilled man. He ruined a slate panel through loss of control of the chisel. I asked acidly if he was well. "Ach, Jonah", he replied roughly, "it's that bugger Russell-Plas-Penrhyn. He was on the phone all bloody night to Moscow of all places. Wouldn't take no for an answer. I got through in the end and he was happy. But I didn't get a wink all night!''

When the news came out, I could forgive all. For a quarter of an hour we felt world famous in the workshop, then I went to the slate works to get another panel. As for the portrait of Bertie, like Epstein I failed to catch the imp in him. But still, I had shaken the hand that had shaken the hand that . . . .

John Cowper Powys (1956)

John Cowper Powys

With the poet Raymond Garlick and a few others, I contributed to a radio broadcast symposium on the great writer John Cowper Powys. I had always admired his work after reading *Glastonbury Romance* in my twenties and at one stage I revelled in a sort of Powys cult surrounding the three literary brothers, John, Llewelyn and Theodore. From photographs it was evident that all the brothers, including Littleton and the expatriate Willie who farmed in Kenya, had magnificent heads. But when Raymond, who then lived in Blaenau Ffestiniog not far from John, introduced us, I was astounded. John occupied a tiny quarryman's cottage, Number One Waterloo Place, one room up and one down, hardly any more. His devoted friend Phyllis Playter looked after him, a tiny acolyte whose charming Bostonian accent contrasted with the vintage Blaenau Welsh all round.

Both Raymond and I had a child with us, he their little son Iestyn, I our three-year-old daughter Naomi. (Oddly enough, as I write nearly thirty years on, both children now work together in the Welsh 'soap opera' *Dinas*.) Phyllis ushered us up the narrow staircase into John's room. This was his world now, books all round from floor to ceiling, and he himself sprawling easily on a couch. He was scribbling on a small clip-board, but seemed only too happy to be interrupted. In one corner was an assortment of walking-sticks, each with its own name and personality. With any one of these John would toddle up the hill behind the house by the steeply falling stream, talking to the stick or to the landscape and its particular gods that day.

He was by now semi-invalid ("your old dribbling dotard" as he signed his letters to Louis Wilkinson sometimes). But when he spoke, one sensed the subterranean energy, the growl of a far from spent volcano. Some people these days would unabashedly call him beautiful. He certainly was, in a strong, noble way. Tall and gangling, his great patrician head covered with white curls, he was the embodiment of the Romano-Celt, if such a figure can exist. It was the fine brow, knitted with thought; the small penetrating eyes with an odd cast; the long, thin-boned nose; and the firm mouth with long upper lip. There were intimations in that face of enormous pent-up energy, even in that strong upper lip a trace of sadism (a subject on which he writes personally as though it were some incubus). Yet he was a totally lovable man. He was the sort of man about whom you could have no reservations. I had loved him through his writings. To meet him was to be committed to him. I asked him if I might make a portrait of him and he replied 'Yes' eagerly, like a boy promised a treat. His whole bearing reminded me of Charlie Chaplin who, when asked on reaching the age of eighty if he felt his age, replied that he woke every morning feeling like a boy with a tree to climb.

John made much of the infants, easily entering their world, and only Miss Playter's reminder that he tired easily tore us away. As for the bust, I knew then it would be only one sitting, hardly worth the trouble. John told me there was already one portrait bust of him — "somewhere in America, I suppose. The last I saw of it was Theodore Dreiser walking down a New York street with it under his arm!" I have often wondered who made that portrait, and if it is still in existence.

So a week later I struggled up the stairs with tripod, clay, bust-peg and small daughter (the latter a condition imposed by John). As they burbled at each other, things were hardly propitious for any sort of portrait. I had an hour or two only to make or break it. Gradually I brought them to order, John back to his couch, Naomi entertaining Miss Playter.

Before we began on the portrait, John insisted on a prayer. Taking up a Greek drachma from the small side table he invoked the Goddess Athene in Greek and then settled down. I pummelled the clay on in fistfuls, half-listening to that wonderful voice, which never paused. He was quite irrepressible. For some reason that day he waxed enthusiastic about Tennyson and he certainly opened my eyes to a poet from whom I had suffered at school along with countless others (all that *Lady of Shalott* business!) and whom I regarded as Victorian and out of fashion, therefore negligible. But John recited whole passages from *Morte d'Arthur*. He could have held huge audiences, indeed he had in his time in America where, he claimed, his notorious stomach ulcer began, leaving him now on a thin diet mostly of raw eggs.

> So all day long the noise of battle rolled
> Along the mountains by the Western shore . . .

he intoned, in a voice of rare resonance and measured rhythm. John belonged to that tireless band of talented hams who have held American audiences in thrall, Dylan Thomas and Vernon Watkins having died of it, while W.H. Auden rode the storm and wrote of his audiences:

> God bless the lot of them, although
> I don't remember which was which:
> God bless the U.S.A, so large,
> So friendly, and so rich.

Occasionally John would break off and make up some nonsense — what his old friend Louis Wilkinson called "his vein of irreverent knock-about buffoonery". The odd thing was that John seemed unconscious of the power of his own voice, its magic, but spoke admiringly of Louis's, to whom he once wrote: "It's your voice when you're on the wireless. Your voice beats mine entirely. Mine is the voice of the actor, an orator, a reciter, a *Preacher*, but yours is the voice of a great Monarch. It is unique. Absolutely unique. So must have been the voice of Xerxes, of Caesar Augustus, of King Solomon . . . ".

Almost perversely, I felt I had something of him in the pummelled clay as he tired himself and I stopped in mid-air. Miss Playter had warned me and I obeyed out of love and I left him quite abruptly. That was the only sitting. I left the clay as it was, took the mould and sent the cast off to the foundry at once. Sometimes I think it is my best portrait, probably because it was the sitter who had signalled when to stop.

Twenty-five years after his death, a group of friends asked me to put up a plaque on Number One Waterloo Place, for they tell me that people still arrive from all over the world to see the small cottage where a great man ended his days.

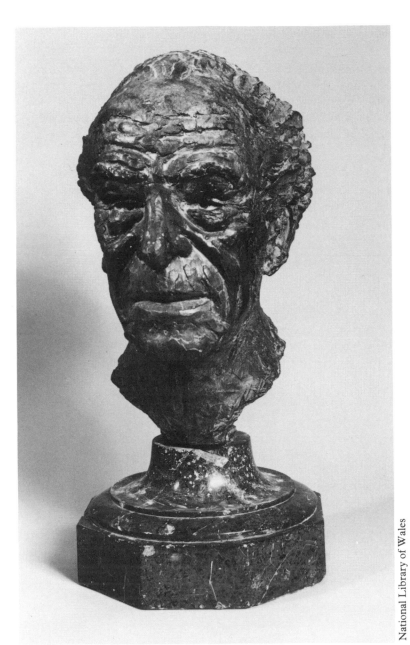

Clough Williams-Ellis (1968)

Clough Williams-Ellis

The winter of 1977–8 was hard on Clough Williams-Ellis, but he would have been the first to declare it had been worse for most of his contemporaries. A few weeks before his death he slipped on ice and fractured his femur, a frequent injury in the old. He knocked himself unconscious and was at once taken to Bangor by ambulance. As the vehicle passed through Penygroes, he came round, asked where he was, and ordered the nurse to take him back home. Of course, with such a helpless casualty the nurse had no choice but to persist with the journey. At hospital in the intensive care unit, Clough turned his face to the wall, refusing to co-operate or to eat. He was beyond what doctors can offer — except that when Lady Amabel (as she was always known towards the end) informed him there was a fifty-fifty chance of success if he was operated on, 'Yes' was the prompt reply. The operation was a success, Clough was returned home according to his wish and in very short time he was receiving friends again at Plas Brondanw, and even toddling about his room on an aluminium 'pulpit'.

A week before he died, I managed with his secretary to help him outside, where he and I sat in a rare hour of April sunshine, sipping sherry before lunch. That was Clough, exulting in the sun, reminiscing and reprimanding, laughing and for a few moments even singing. I had not known he was a connoisseur of twenties' hits. We tripped heavily (given the awful timbre of our respective voices) through one or two Coward numbers. He remembered the words better than I did. Tone deaf as we both were, the Master would have been horrified.

We expressed gratitude for the bright morning after the rigours of a hard winter. Weather had always fascinated both of us. On our estuary, a good day, winter or summer, was a matter for exultation, but in summer it was sheer heaven, never oppressive even at the hottest. Every autumn he and I assessed the foregoing summer, rather like examining undergraduates for their degrees. It began in 1959 — "To the summer of 1959" he wrote and I inscribed on a disc of Portland Stone, "in honour of its splendour". If the summer were not worth discussion, we tactfully ignored it and waited with a lifetime's purview. We had a long wait at first. The gay sixties were nothing to write home about weatherwise. Did weather matter in those heady days when even the implacable General de Gaulle had to bend to the wind of change? Incidentally, I recall Clough chortling with me once over a 'Grauniad' misprint in 1956 during the Suez crisis — "General de Gaulle and Colonel Nasser exchanged massages".

So, the weather was declared delightful that bright April morning. The singing came to an end, whether for want of breath or repertoire I would not care to say. He suddenly quietened, then declared, provocatively: "I've decided after all these years that I'm an atheist!" I loved him for that, because of the courage, defiance and, of course, the implicit doubt of seven or eight decades, for his father, having been of the cloth, must at the very least have initiated the internal argument, and Clough had at long last decided against, at a moment when you might expect the opposite.

His monument, of course, is Portmeirion, or Porthmeirion as it is now called. I am not sure he would have approved of that, however much we espouse the cause of correct Welsh (and insofar as I'm able I do), for there is a nostalgic archaism about the bad Welsh, rather like the 'Festiniog Railway' nearby, a relic of the English or Anglicised Welsh ascendancy of the eighteenth and nineteenth centuries.

Puritanical critics might decry Portmeirion, but he built it with passionate conviction and very little money. It is among the most enjoyable things around these days in a very naughty world as far as environment goes. John Cowper Powys, in a letter to Louis Wilkinson, described it well, if with faulty nomenclature!: " . . . the most extraordinary place three or four miles large along the sea shore called Port Merrion & built or invented by that daring Architect Mister William Clough-Ellis. Phyllis describes it as a Ballet Stage Setting on the everlasting Sands of Time . . . . It is a Faked-Antiquity or Pseudo-Romance, but the more intelligent you are the more you cotton to it. It's like a 'Folly' in the time of Horace Walpole painted by Gainsborough. Fake-Fake Pseudo-Pseudo, but so highly decorative that it is like some Petit Trianon of Versailles — False light, fake pseudo airy fairy, but a pure pleasure!"

Like most cultural attractions, Portmeirion is suffering today from the very tourists it attracts, as with Florence or the

Parthenon, all in danger of being trampled into the ground by the sheer numbers of their admirers. Portmeirion's buildings, set in their particular verdant dell by a tidal estuary, were never meant to be seen against such crowds, and I remember, shortly after the war, painting the sign for Clough which read: "In order that visitors to Portmeirion be kept to an acceptable number a toll of 'so-and-so' (it varied according to the season) will be charged". But the sign and the toll in those days did keep numbers to an 'acceptable' level. Not so today, when One Pound, Two Pounds, are not too much, we pay each other so well these days. The ease of transport makes everything so very accessible, and only the tragic accident to the NASA shuttle has delayed the crowding of outer space with hordes of tourists aiming their Hasselblads at Mother Earth. Yet the paradox in all this is that Portmeirion would probably fall down but for the tourist income. The maintenance of property is an expensive business these days.

Clough favoured the theatrical over real life. In details he would often prefer a 'dodge' to a formal solution. Who else but he would think of erecting tin cut-outs to represent obelisks and statues? Yet his employment of Hans Feibusch the mural painter is also an example of his enlightened patronage, for nothing is so characteristic of Portmeirion as Feibusch's work, where it has survived. In the early days he employed an enlightened master of lettering, Ralph Ellis, a first World War contemporary, and it is sad that so little of his work has survived.

Even the scale of Portmeirion is just that little less than one thinks. You find yourself stooping slightly to negotiate an arch that, from a distance, appears to be in firm human scale but it is in fact just a little less. I believe this was not so much a matter of economy (he was not rich and had no illusions that PM was a self-indulgence), as to accommodate the fabric to the confines of the narrow dell in which the village is sited.

Alas, the hotel itself, which was an extended version of the original house of Aber Iâ, is no longer, having been gutted by fire one wild June night in 1981. Its restoration will contain very little of his various extensions to the house, but that is no great fault since the original Victorian elevation, set hard by the shore, is unique and intrinsically attractive.

Visitors to the grounds will have their favourite features, vintage examples of Clough's craft, or more likely of his magpie instinct for collecting fragments or whole fabrics of demolished structures. My own favourite is the Colonnade, a Bath Stone

The Colonnade at Portmeirion

edifice from Bristol which had been an eighteenth century Bath House, then a tram stop. As usual, Clough described this in his inimitable baroque style on the plaques under its cover:

> This Colonnade built circa 1760 by the Quaker copper smelter William Reeve, stood before his bath house at Arnos Court, Bristol. Damaged by bombs it had fallen into decay and although scheduled as an ancient monument Her Majesty's Minister of Works approved its removal on condition that it should be here rescheduled.
>
> Admired by its alert contemporary Horace Walpole for its grace as a Classical Composition enriched by Gothick detail it was also held in high esteem by the Council for the Preservation of Ancient Bristol whose good offices and the generosity of its former owners, the Bristol Tramways and Carriage Company, have made possible its preservation at Portmeirion.

He had a happy knack at writing out inscriptions, and any at Portmeirion are worth pausing at to read. Indeed, his prose style in general matches his building style and his several books deserve to be remembered on their own merits.

At either end of the Colonnade, an ogee cupola is supported on two corbels. One of these was missing when the drivers off-loaded, so Clough asked me to carve one out of a blank in its place. He gave me very little time, as usual, and I carved, as I thought, a sketch portrait of Clough. It looks to me more like Noel Coward, who would have 'simply adored' the idea of supporting an ogee cupola in Portmeirion, where he wrote *Blithe Spirit*.

Portmeirion started off as a fine dream and it was gradually eroded, by life, by time, and by the gradual contraction of all our dreams following the war. The original intention that it should provide a retreat for artists and writers soon faded, artists and writers being what they are, refusing to conform, chary of arranged retreats and preferring to search out their own or even fleeing from any idea of retreat.

Clough was great fun. He enjoyed the macabre and belonged to that rare breed like Horace Walpole and Peacock who kept a foot in both the Classical and the Romantic worlds. I would place Clough with a few rare spirits among the best company to enjoy. He wrote as felicitously as he drew and built, and perhaps he talked even better. What is unique about him is that he looked like Clough, stalking through the gardens on his long thin legs clad in britches and yellow stockings without the least affectation.

He loved Wales passionately. He was early in the moves to

designate National Parks. It was typical of him when he was showing George VI round Eryri that he should point up to the peak of Snowdon with his cane and say, in answer to a Royal query: "Actually that bit belongs to me but you can keep that under your crown".

His defiance of architectural trends is in many ways now justified. Many of his buildings, like Capel Moriah at Llanystumdwy, stand the test of time better than most contemporary buildings. Nor was his design necessarily expensive. At one period in his career, he declared he could build a worker's cottage for one hundred and ten pounds and it was true at the time and he did it. He was a great patron of the young and I owed a great deal to his patronage when I returned from army service and sought to establish myself as artist and craftsman in Gwynedd in those austere post-war years.

He had all the qualities required for life. He was an indefatigable survivor. He was foolish enough in the First World War to volunteer to man a captive balloon for artillery spotting, an easy target for the enemy. Who but he could survive a serious car accident in his late eighties? He was well liked by men and adored of women. He loved nature and its gentle submission to the ministrations of a sympathetic gardener or architect, and he had the good sense to grasp what opportunities life offered him and to make the most of them. But most of all, I think, he had that grotesque sense of humour, of spoof. For example, how is one to take the inscription under the Bell Tower: "This tower, built in 1928 by Clough Williams-Ellis, Architect and Publican, embodies stones from the 12th Century Castle of his Ancestor Gruffydd ap Cynan King of North Wales that stood on an eminence 150 yards to the west. It was finally razed c.1869 by Sir Wm Fothergill Cook inventor of the Electric Telegraph 'lest the ruins should become known and attract visitors to the place'. This 19th century affront to the 12th is thus piously redressed in the 20th"? One imagines Clough the publican drawing pints for his thirsty Celtic ancestor Gruffydd ap Cynan while a bouncer throws out Sir Wm Fothergill Cook.

He treated death as lightly as he treated life. Discussing with the late Lady Aberconway how he could get her ashes into an urn on top of a tall column he planned to build for her, the reply was prompt — "There will be a tube from bottom to top and we'll blow them up by bellows." His last wish was that his own ashes should be sent up by rocket over the beautiful Dwyryd estuary. I never walk there at low tide without saying to myself: "Here lies

Clough."

Losing him was one of those rare moments when I knew what all that monarch and Elvis adulation is about — I'd lost my King, and I know many of his friends share that loss. He left a world of mediocrity, and like him, we must care as passionately about the world and our neighbours if we are to turn up the light just that little.

The day before he died, Clough still managed to steal the show. He loved to quote fatuous lines like "backing into the limelight". Another favourite was that such and such body was "a hotbed of cold feet". BBC 2 visited me one day to record my impressions of another neighbour, Richard Hughes, or Diccon, as we all knew him. I completed my stint, then asked whom they were seeing next. "Lady Amabel", they replied. Amabel did indeed know as much as anybody about Diccon's early days. When the crew got to Plas Brondanw, they found Clough sprawling on a couch, obviously not far from death, and dozing. But the sight of a camera or recording outfit would alert him to the very end. He declared he had something to say about Diccon. A few months later, while we were still feeling the pain of his departure, tears pricked my eyes as we heard that booming voice from the grave, speaking most eloquently on his impressions of Diccon. It was as he would have wished, to go out working to the very end, still backing into the limelight. After that recording he relapsed into sleep and never woke again, unless in some Portmeirion in the heaven in which he firmly did not believe — or did he?

That is something we never know of one another — where we stand *sub specie aeternitatis*. But I cannot resist appending a letter written late in his life to another peninsular eccentric, Captain Henry Winch, dated November 25, 1971.

Thanks for notice dear Henry — but Harlech Meeting on the 4th Dec — Alas! not possible, I think (Amabel in London at moment) But we shall scarcely be back in time from Devon — where that day a monument of mine is being dedicated by the Arch Bish of Canterbury. A 4 engined jet is touching down for us at Llanbedr (with his Grace on board!) & will deliver us back that evening.
We should make the headlines if we crash!
    yrs
      Clough.

Huw Wheldon (1979)

Huw Wheldon

The one thing I remember most forcibly about making a portrait bust of Huw Wheldon was that it was great fun. I modelled it at his home on Richmond Hill, and amid his bouts of busyness over BBC or the London School of Economics (he was supposed to be retired but remained a constant adviser to both till the end) he would say: "Shall we have a few fragrant moments, then?" and sit down and patiently abide my attempts to capture that extraordinarily volatile countenance in clay.

He was among our oldest friends, so that was fun too. Both my wife and I had known him from Army days, he and I from service in the 6th Airborne Division and my wife from Middle East service in the ATS. We all foregathered, after hostilities ceased, as members of the Educational Corps at Number One Army Formation College on Mount Carmel in what was then called Palestine, under the British Mandate. The college buildings themselves were my wife's old Reali School, commandeered by our Army. We were drafted there in the name of Education, either to lecture in our various capacities or to get in a month or so of study to prepare for a return to undergraduate life after demobilisation. In some ways I would place that particular Army initiative as one of the sources of the subsequent Open University, with which Huw was later very much concerned. Carmel College was also great fun, not least because of the inimitable laughter of the great man himself, for even then he was easily distinguished in the crowd in the Mess. He would be the cynosure, with intermittent gales of laughter radiating outwards like a tidal wave. So making a portrait of him thirty-five years later was bound to be fun.

He was the least pompous big man I have ever met. At the most formative period of television he had tremendous power in the constant search to promote excellence and to achieve what is sometimes called vulgarly 'spread'. Quality versus ratings, I suppose. Excellence he insisted on, yet he never lost the common touch. He was just as much at home over dinner with a debauch of dons at Peterhouse as he was on the Criccieth Golf Course in Caernarfonshire, "playing exceedingly bad golf with extremely good chaps!" (He was a master of the emphatic adverb.) Either occasion would be made hilarious by his presence. His self-deprecation was not some sort of cover for deficiencies, be they in intellect or in golf (and he was far from deficient in either) — no, it was simply fun. In the name of fun he would recount his worst failings, like the story of school at Friars in Bangor, and the marks for some subject being read out by the master: — "Evans, J.H., 4 out of 10, must try harder; Williams, P., 5 out of 10, still not good enough, I'm afraid; Wheldon, H.P., 2 out of 10, a great improvement." What he would not mention was that he excelled at English, was one of its greatest speaking exponents. Not that he ever made any claims to academic distinction — indeed quite the opposite. He would say how little he had made of his education. Possibly, as with so many sons of strong characters, this was partly due to being the son of a distinguished academic, Sir Wynn.

Huw believed passionately in excellence when it came to public service, in the need to recognise and nurture it. That was his vocation, to search it out and promote it wherever he could find it. He had learned the job, with those two principal criteria of excellence and of public accessibility to it, from his first post-war job as Director of the Welsh Committee of the Arts Council of Great Britain. Thence he went on to the Festival of Britain, which he helped organise (including a concert by Horowitz — there's excellence for you), and finally to the BBC, his true home, where he soon found himself on the ladder to the top. It was as though the medium had been waiting for his like. Many a well-known TV figure today owes his or her beginnings to his nurturing and many a programme of excellence can be traced back to his influence.

Among his many qualities I would rate highly his genius as a story teller. He was the best conversationalist I have ever known. He could string out the simplest story and never bore you — he was incapable of boring. He would never talk of his war, except for one tale which I remember enjoying. The 6th Airborne Division landing in Normandy was quite a shambles, as airborne landings usually are. Huw told the story of being in charge of a glider with a small artillery piece and twenty men to land somehow. The glider was towed, of course, by a plane, usually a Dakota, Stirling or Halifax, and once over the dropping zone, the glider cast off the tow-rope while the plane returned to safety at home base, leaving the glider to fend as best it could. Huw told of the dreadful ensuing silence, the rapid descent into hostile Normandy, the bumping and boring of the actual landing. But they landed well enough, and it was then Huw's task to off-load the gun and muster the men in the best military order and to be ready for action at once.

As he told the tale, he evoked the air of men at the ready, gun loaded, only sight and sound of the enemy wanting for battle to commence. It was all in the middle of a midsummer night (June 5/6th) of course, so visibility was not at all bad. Having done everything according to the correct drill, but without any sign of an enemy to engage, the problem for a young officer in charge was what to do next, for no Allied presence was evident either. Huw had the capacity to hold you as he told a tale, until you were breathless to hear the next step. Well, he and his troop had reached this dreadful pulsating silence, apparently all alone on a midsummer night in hostile territory, with neither friend nor enemy apparent. What next? Well, said Huw, the next thing he heard was the noise of twenty men standing against the nearest hedge, having a pee — and follows the great laugh.

What he would never recount was how, next day in full daylight, having discovered they were in the neighbourhood of a German Panzer Division, he withdrew his men safely, to rendezvous with the Division again, a difficult feat for which he was awarded the Military Cross. Beyond that funny story I never heard him talk of the war.

Trying to recapture the mood and substance of his conversation is extraordinarily difficult. So much depended on the delivery and the spontaneity, *and* the company. I do not recall any immortal 'one-liners', but rather, particularly *en famille*, a rollicking sense of fun. It would appear silly in print and in some ways, had he had a Boswell, the poor biographer would have been lost for something actually to put down. Much of it was simply fatuous. For example, the two families took a long walk, a traverse from Tan-y-Grisiau, up over Cwmorthin and down into Cwm Croesor, as fine a walk as you could wish in the hills of Meirionnydd. From something our daughter Naomi said, Huw promptly renamed her 'Ann Ffurfiol' (from the Welsh *anffurfiol* — 'informal'). Now why this should produce gales of laughter I don't know, but the 'script', so to speak, continued throughout the walk, with all the permutations of what a young girl called Ann Ffurfiol would be likely to do. Once we all climbed Manod Mawr near Ffestiniog. It began to rain stair-rods and we descended in a hurry, soaked to the skin, crowded like sardines into the Mini and in no time the little car was steaming like a laundry and smelling worse. "Frightfully foetid in here, don't you think," said Huw, "in fact, a quite considerable fet". A *fet* henceforth entered the family vocabulary.

Now all this is only the private nonsense of a public figure, and neither gives the flavour of the man, nor seems worth recording. Yet Boswell did in fact experience much the same thing in trying to pin down what it was in Johnson that riveted audiences. Under *Aetat 70* he records how a foreign minister "of no very high talents", suffering neglect somewhat in the master's company, plucked up courage and piped in with his own admiration of *The Rambler*, which Johnson took up with: "The Ambassadour says well . . . ". "And many a time afterwards", Boswell records, "it furnished a pleasant topick of merriment: 'The Ambassadour says well,' became a laughable term of applause, when no mighty matter had been expressed."

But of course there was much more to Huw than that. That is all for some future biographer who will, I presume, be able to assess his contribution to the development of television. Huw was incisive in argument, decisive in action but above all strong in presence. Of Huw's ultimate status in that strange new world of temporary and lasting fame, there can be no doubt. He made no bones about it himself, declaring with becoming modesty: "I do like glory, don't you?"

Yet in one or two respects we differed strangely. First, on Welshness he was staunch. He was a Welshman of that 'club' of Welsh-speaking Welsh, and of that he would allow no doubt whatsoever. He was proud of it and grateful for it. It was a thing he cherished. His grandfather had been a prominent preacher in Ffestiniog and his father was a great and much respected educationist. Yet when our children took up the cause in the seventies of *Y Gymdeithas yr Iaith Gymraeg* (The Welsh Language Society), Huw was deeply offended. I think the gratuitous vandalism that was involved occasionally and the intimations that it might turn into some sort of minor Welsh terror, upset him. He loved the language deeply and he felt the demonstrations at the time brought it down rather than raised it. I felt he was wrong, but I was not in a position to argue, since my own learned Welsh is so poor.

The second area of difference was barely mentioned between us, though it was there towards the end of his life. He espoused the beliefs of what is called neo-conservatism, especially that of his close friend in America, Norman Podhoretz and the *Commentary* magazine. I never understood this. Huw had been brought up in the old Welsh traditions, he had been educated at the London School of Economics. For me that implied Harold Laski and radical rather than conservative approaches to politics. I have never felt any urge to change the early political attitudes gained in my upbringing, while I feel Huw did change. A friendship like that between our two families can ride such differences with ease, and I would be the first to admit I can offer very little wisdom on the subject of politics.

There are few things in life that move one so deeply that they seem beyond bearing or telling; perhaps the death of a parent, the birth of a grandchild, the giving away of a daughter in marriage. But outside that, I believe the most moving thing I remember in a life dedicated to family, friendship and art was the sound of Miss Jessye Norman singing Handel's *Zadok the Priest* in Wesminster Abbey at Huw's Memorial Service. The BBC Symphony Orchestra played in the great crossing, the congregation sat all round and the Abbey was full. Paul Fox, another old friend and colleague dating back to Army days, had delivered the panegyric and there was a momentary silence. Then came the click of feminine heels over the Abbey flags and this magnificent woman stood in our midst, monumental in her stance, the pale ebony of her face rapt with the prospect of music. The orchestra struck a chord and Miss Norman burst into song. As she projected her voice into the vast nave, the tears poured down my cheeks, quite uncontrollably. It was not only that Huw would have been moved too (he loved Handel). It was also the sheer sound of that voice, that magnificent instrument, its power and beauty, of that order which makes you realise that however good modern reproduction methods may be, nothing can ever capture the vibrancy, timbre and clarity of the human voice at its best. It was one of the most beautiful experiences in my life. Later, as we filed out of the Abbey, I noticed Miss Norman standing to one side at the door, waiting for a friend. Nothing would have been easier than to stretch out a hand to shake hers and to thank her. But I was incapable of speech. I think I would have broken down. All this Huw would have understood.

It was typical of him that in his will he should leave to each of twelve special chums "a dozen bottles of claret of reasonable quality" and I was proud and grateful to be among them, smiling with him as he would have intended, I have no doubt. As ever, he was louder than life.

Richard Hughes

Richard Hughes

There was a levity about Richard Hughes's high seriousness that could be very off-putting. Take the second novel *In Hazard*, a tale about a near shipwreck in a hurricane in the Caribbean. Inevitably it is compared with Conrad's great novella *Typhoon*. Now about the latter there is never any doubt about its high seriousness. The entire novella is doom-laden. The roaring typhoon is hell-bent on the destruction of the ship, the crew bear up under the most appalling strain against all that the gods can fling at them. Conrad often reminds you of Hercules bearing the whole world on his shoulders, and though I love him dearly, I wish sometimes he would release us from his almost perpetual Heart of Darkness. Once, writing to Bertrand Russell about Socialism, Conrad declared: "I have never been able to find in any man's talk anything convincing enough to stand up for a moment against my deep-seated sense of fatality governing this man-inhabited earth".

Now nobody could accuse Richard Hughes of that. Shortly after his untimely death (he had seemed still young of heart at seventy not long previous, but leukemia is a dread reducer of the persona) a group of us recorded a BBC2 broadcast in his memory. I recall quoting from *In Hazard* the image of the pet lemur on board the *Archimedes*, or the 'Madagascar Cat' as it was called, 'Tom' who, at the height of the storm is engaged on lifting the eyelid of the Mate, Mr Rabb, huddled flaked-out below decks:

> Thomas, with the absorption of a handicraftsman, his own nocturnal eyes glowing like lamps in the light of the torch, was endeavouring to pick those clamped eyelids open again in vain.

There was something of this curious cat about Diccon (as we knew him), a sardonic observer of the human condition, always with a wry smile shining through what might appear as a forbidding exterior to some. He stalked his estate on the far shore of our estuary, Traeth Bach, summoning up images that refused to crystallise, or so it seemed, for he was in perpetual conflict with his Muse.

"What are you busy with, Diccon?" one might innocently ask, for is it not always a matter of curiosity to readers enthralled by such masterpieces as *High Wind, In Hazard* and the *Fox in the Attic* trilogy which a recalcitrant Muse refused to allow him to complete?

"Today? I took out a comma and inserted a full stop," he would answer. Nobody seemed so secretive about the creative process. You might arrive at the house, *Mor Edrin*, hard by the eastern shore of Traeth Bach, and his secretary might be leaving the house with a few papers under her arm, as though in flight. That might be *it*, the month's instalment towards *The Fox*, but you would never know. Whatever it was, it would be a different view of humanity, possibly eccentric but hard-hitting and right on target, like the portrait of Emily in *High Wind*. That novel, surely, exploded the myth of those little darlings, children.

> Take that curious opposition, and tension (or at least tie), which exists in all men, and indeed in all beasts, between parent and child. The form in which it emerges into behaviour is (broadly speaking) a matter of cultural environment. Amongst Anglo-Saxons, it flowers for the most part in revolt: in an exaggerated contempt of the adolescent child for the parent: a contempt far greater than he would feel for any other human being of the same calibre as his father. (*In Hazard*)

One would imagine he had the most appalling relationship with his own children, but the converse was true. Nevertheless he had no illusions. Even children's incipient sexuality, a taboo subject, emerges in the most fastidious way. Take that opening to *The Wooden Shepherdess*, the meeting between Augustine and Ree:

> Then — with her eyelids still shut so tight that they quivered — her hand fumbled open the front of his shirt and slid right inside, warm against skin still froggy a bit from the creek: "Sakes!" she exclaimed. "What makes your heart hammer so?"
>   Firmly he felt for those fingers and gently withdrew them: let go the moment he got them outside . . .

Diccon was unorthodox, unabashed and uninhibited. I recall one young woman friend telling me of the shock of her first encounter with him as a child. There was quite a party, grown-ups and children, and Diccon took them sailing across the fair waters of the Traeth. Then, since it was a hot day, Diccon decided it was time for a swim. Off came his clothes and he dived overboard. "Can you imagine the shock?" said my friend, "I was only eleven or so and it was the first time I'd seen a man's balls."

Yet the last thing you could accuse Diccon of was 'kinkiness', though I've heard the accusation made. Diccon behaved with impeccable rectitude where morality is concerned. He was a good Anglican, not that that is necessarily a criterion. It was simply that he had no illusions about human nature — that may be why the late and partly aborted masterpiece *The Fox* was to be called *The Human Predicament*. It would never have occurred to him to question nudity, and if shock was involved, then so be it. He knew what is not generally recognised, that the normal, healthy child is tough and resilient of mind and body. The message of *High Wind* is clear — do not take that loving dependence of our offspring for granted. The moment something attractive turns up alternative to our parents' perpetual surveillance, like a bit of amiable piracy, we are soon forgotten. If that be an exaggeration, is not all the best fiction something of that? We may never know a Julien Sorel or an Emma Bovary in the flesh, yet are they not paradigms of people we have met?

Certainly my wife and I never had any qualms about sending our children over if he wanted to see them, as he did from time to time. "I'm seventy today," he once telephoned, "and I want your children to come over." "But how," my wife asked, "Jonah is at work and has the car." "I'll come over on the horse" he replied, "and fetch them. I want to play charades for my birthday." And that was that. The children padded down to the edge of the water, horse and rider turned up on the far side, the horse negotiated the stream which at low tide is sometimes no more than two feet deep, and they were off, for a day's charades and high jinks in and around *Mor Edrin*, with Frances, his wife, smiling at the whole affair and preparing a groaning board of imaginative viands fit for a Diccon party. Our eldest son was once so taken with one of her dishes that he turned to her and said "This is so good I could kiss you till you are wet all over!" Diccon would have loved that.

And beyond reading every word of his, from the early collection of verse *Confessio Juvenis* onwards, that was all I was really to know of Diccon. Our relationship was, so to speak, trans-estuarine, and never came to more than that. I never made a portrait of him and perhaps I was right, because in that unique bare room soaked in the light from the estuary, one of Augustus John's better portraits had caught the quintessential Diccon to a T.

It says something of the pull of literature that, in retrospect, I am prepared to put up with that limitation. What I can never forgive is the way the Muse withheld that last of the late trilogy (and God knows he waited for years). After *The Wooden Shepherdess* . . . what? We shall never know. Even his daughter Penelope, who was closest to that part of him and communed most with him over the difficulties and has written superbly of that relationship, even she could not carry on with it from what notes he left. There was an attempt in a radio broadcast, but we shall never know. Diccon's was a unique imagination, and though works more recent like Paul Theroux's *Mosquito Coast* echo some of *High Wind*'s lost innocence, Diccon was the forerunner, the first to lift our sleeping eyelids to uncover the weird dreams, imaginings and fantasies that lurk at the back of the mind of even the most innocent.

Not Built But Truly Born

I was busy fixing my bust of Bob Tai'r Felin the ballad singer to its appropriate plinth of a millstone. Since it was the Easter holidays I had a van-load of children with me, but despite the crowd, the nearest farmhouse bade us have tea with them. While the children cleared the board three times over my eyes scanned the walls of the low room. "Heb Fam, Heb Cartref" I read, carved on a piece of oak, unsigned but dated 1933 — "it's no place without Mother". A trite enough homily — but true even so. It was a nice bit of carved lettering — what in the trade would be called 'sunk-raised'. But among all the normal and amusing things that adorned the walls of that Welsh farmhouse, one thing took my eye. The place sparkled, but this item more than anything. It was an ordinary spring balance, the kind used for weighing a flitch of bacon. It had a dial of burnished brass and it hung from the wall by a gleaming steel hook. Below it hung another highly polished hook, to take the burden of bacon, corn or whatever they weigh on these things. I suppose it had been used for weighing, but it had long given up such earthly labours. It was obviously now an object of daily domestic attention, even a sort of devotion. Yet why? What is there about an ordinary spring balance for weighing bacon that would excite devotion in a Welsh farmhouse? It is not exactly a fine piece of machinery; the pointer says vaguely 13 or 14 pounds and wobbles accordingly as your arm aches. No, it wasn't the mechanism. It was the brightness, that capacity for burnishing. That brass dial and those steel hooks shone with a glory that a finger would have sullied.

And I remembered that in the kitchen of Twm Williams of Pentrefelin, who built the masonry substructure for the Bob Tai'r Felin memorial, there was another wall-piece — what can one call it? This one was no more, and no less, than the chromium-plated hub-cap that had fallen from some passing car. This too gleamed with an almost holy light and with the brass spring balance it was typical of many an old-fashioned

Welsh kitchen.

Now I have tried to understand this, for the balance and the hub-cap are palpable images or objects, and my own job is concerned mostly with the making of palpable images. When I see them I always think — if only I could create a piece of sculpture that could compel such daily attention. What is it that attracts the housewife in these almost meaningless objects? Primarily I suppose their response to her touch, her elbow. They register, somewhat aggressively, her devotion to cleanliness. She is so devoted to it, bless her, that I want to carve on the slate chimney-breast 'Godliness is next to Cleanliness'.

The very emptiness of these shining ikons of brass is indicative. Do they fill a gap, like one notorious Sunday newspaper? I can't think of another answer. After all, the floor, the table-top, every simple object in the room is witness to the energy of that elbow, and central to the whole complex, and special, is the gleaming balance or hub-cap. It is nearly always useless and unnecessary — redundant. It would be better, surely, if it had some meaning, some use, however small. I feel it occupies a place comparable to the ikons that once occupied (still do, I believe) a central place in Russian homes. They are a sort of touchstone, a sign manual that life goes on and is upheld.

But their emptiness of meaning too is a sign. If their burnished brightness asserts firm domestic rule, their lack of content betrays an atrophy of part of the human spirit. For all through the ages, and among all peoples, small images have been made and have held the devotion of households, the *lares* or household gods of the Latins. They have figured so importantly that tiny domestic images have survived from civilisations as remote as Ur or the kingdoms of the Nile. The canopas of the Incas are evidence too, outside our own Mediterranean complex of civilisations.

Recently I was asked if there was evidence of a renaissance in the visual arts in Wales. The answer is No. Renaissance means rebirth, the resuscitation of something fine that once existed but has virtually lapsed over a period of time. And if one compares the surviving iconography of Wales over a thousand years with that of other civilisations, there is precious little to show. The Welsh, if they are not iconoclasts, certainly have not been the most active of image-makers, and one cannot therefore talk of the renaissance of what has never really existed. When the archaeologists dig up the buried civilisations of Ur, Egypt, Greece, Pompeii, they find countless precious and often beautiful images. I think particularly of the little terracotta images from Tanagra in Greece. These homely little objects, images of daily life, were found in cemeteries dating from three or four centuries before Christ. They give us a very clear picture of contemporary life and there is one splendid group in the British Museum of two women gossiping. Sadly, historic Welsh sites like Deganwy or Aberffraw yield nothing, or at best very little. The old Celts travelled very light. The archaeologists of the future may be puzzled when they find in a typical Welsh kitchen a spring balance or a hub-cap as the centre piece. What will scholars make of them? Objects of veneration? Ikons, abstract in design? Domestic utensils of enhanced value? A form of currency, like Old Masters?

I think it is safe to generalise and to declare that the Welsh have been comparatively devoid of image-makers, and to talk of a renaissance is a false assumption. Images do exist, of course, and I use the adverb 'comparatively' with the wealth of remains of certain other peoples in mind. It does not signify a deficiency in the Welsh. As a people the Welsh are devoid neither of energy nor spirit. I state it merely as a fact. For there are reasons for it. In the first place, image-making is not merely the result of a predisposition in a people. Rather is it the result of a happy accident. There would have been no sculpture on the Acropolis had there not been the finest of all stone nearby, the marble of Mount Pentelus. The glories of Rome and Florence and all Italy reflect not only the spirit of a people but also the presence of another great quarry, at Carrara. Even the little Tanagra figurines indicate the presence of a readily available bed of high quality clay. The wonderful Baroque wood-carvings of Bavaria and Austria owe their existence in part to the fine timber, notably lime, that flourishes in those parts of Central Europe.

Now stone, clay and wood exist in Wales, but none of them is readily carvable, none of them *invites* the craftsman to settle down and create an image. Granite, slate and dwarf sessile oak will carve, just — but they do not invite it. What of the basalt and diorite of Egypt? Well, Egypt used granite, yes, but think of the omnipotence of the king and the thousands of slaves. No king could rule Wales, no Welshman could command such servitude, nor submit to it. Mountains preclude it for a start.

The materials of Wales, therefore, can be regarded as inconducive to image-making. But the presence of materials is mere geographical location and accident. The spirit of a people is undaunted by mere absence of materials. If the need is there, something will answer that need. Indeed materials were even exported from Wales, at what pain and effort we cannot imagine, to make Stonehenge. What a colossal urge of the human spirit that must have been, to unearth, transport and erect those vast bluestone monoliths from Preseli. But their austere monumental bareness is sufficient witness to the intractable nature of Welsh stone.

Absence of the right materials is easily demonstrated. But the spirit of a people? How explain the virtual iconoclasm of an entire people? Since I have been talking in comparative terms, let me say that England, though much richer in sculptural materials, in limestone particularly and sandstone and clay, and therefore somewhat richer than Wales in images, falls far below other civilisations. Yet this single move over the border is revealing. For there is a heart to these things, and it lies in the Mediterranean. Just as the climate gets warmer as we near that blue inland sea, so the images get thicker on the ground. Italy is so rich that a whole lifetime could not exhaust the imagery of Rome and Florence alone. From that Mediterranean heart the arteries spread and the pulse gets steadily weaker as they near the extremities.

The question therefore is not "Is there a renaissance of the visual arts in Wales?", but rather whether or not one should expect them to flourish in Wales at all. The answer for the past is, I think, No. Yet, as I suggested earlier, there is a strange need somewhere. If I speak of the past and say No to talk of a renaissance, what then of birth? What of the future? In my experience there are signs of hope. The balance and the Ikon are not without point. No amount of propaganda can make art, least of all a national iconography. The writer Lawrence Durrell makes one of his characters, a novelist, say this — "For the artist, I think, as for the public, no such thing as art exists; it only exists for the critics and those who live in the forebrain". There is something in this. An artist does not rationalise, he is simply a maker, and high talk of art often silences him. An iconography is not premeditated, it simply happens. Art cannot be legislated in Wales, it can be taught, it can be bought, but it cannot be imposed. Yet the meaningless ikons betray a need for visible, palpable expressions of the human spirit in a country starved of them.

Now the humble devotion by the local people in raising a memorial, an image of their own Bob Tai'r Felin of fond memory, was a sign, I think. For this was a purely local effort,

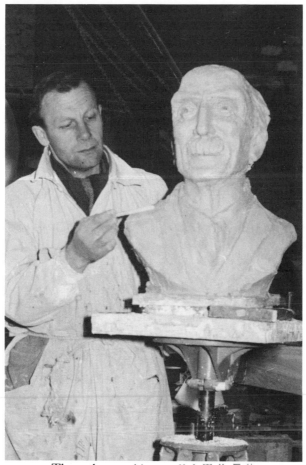
The author working on Bob Tai'r Felin

unsubsidised, barely advertised. The sponsors even urged that
subscriptions should be small — surely a unique plea these days.
The effort did not end, as happens so often, at collecting money
and organising the unveiling. No, they were determined that it
had to be right, appropriate to Bob. For a miller, what more
appropriate than a millstone? That millstone, a perfect example,
still wearing its iron tyre, was lifted, transported, levered and
heaved into place, almost druidically, by local farm workers.
They watched Twm Williams point the cement, rubbed the soil
from their hands, viewed the project critically and pronounced
that it was good. Next day they dropped a fine old stone roller
perilously and even more arduously into the central orifice of the
millstone where it served as a column on which to mount the

head of old Bob. That was my part, the head — but the whole image, the memorial, was the dream and creation of a small locality in Wales. I think it has given me more pleasure than any job I remember, because it *is* a sign. With that local help, and with the local materials, it passed that test so well phrased by the Italian Renaissance historian Vasari — "*Non murato ma veramente nato*" — "not built but truly born".

Bronze figures have been raised in the past I know. But they were the work of architects and sculptors imposed on a public too ready to acquiesce, too nervous to contribute more than the money, too unpractised in the art of iconography to do more than gladly hand the work over to the expert and take whatever he thought right. Wales, heaven knows, has its share of bronze worthies on boring pedestals. I was deeply conscious of this when my turn came to erect a monument. I have tried, in the memorial to O.M. Edwards and his son Syr Ifan in a bold and simple *cilfach* of Arenig granite, and to Bob Tai'r Felin on his farm roller and millstone, to break this outworn tradition not only for my own peace of mind, but at the behest of my sponsors. That is a sign, the sponsors' new awareness.

If one cannot speak of a renaissance, one can cautiously speak of a beginning, for this century has seen several artists of renown in Wales whose work has attracted attention home and abroad and has contributed its drop of precious blood to the arteries that nourish the human spirit.

* * *

Postscript

A considerable amount of my work is on public sites, and therefore has suffered from one of the special ills of our age — vandalism. Sadly, both Bob Tai'r Felin and the Edwards monument at Llanuwchllyn have suffered. During the Cofia Tryweryn (Remember Tryweryn: a Welsh village which was drowned by a reservoir for Liverpool) campaign a transformer on the contractor's site was damaged. The readiest Welsh target for a group of his workers was Bob. He was attacked with bricks and smashed. Later I took away the granite roller and the broken head, and keeping only the original millstone I placed a carved profile of Bob on it. It seems to survive. But nothing is sure these days, alas.

The revised Bob Tai'r Felin Monument (1982)

As for the Llanuwchllyn monument — those who remember both father and son, Syr O.M. and Syr Ifan ab Owen Edwards will recall that the latter was never seen without glasses. Co-operating with the bronze foundry I managed to reproduce those specs to good effect, I believe. They survived only a week or two. Late one Saturday evening, the lads climbed on to the plinth and levered off those vulnerable bronze specs. No point was made, nothing was gained, no cause or protest of any kind was advanced by so doing. It was simply that the glasses were there and were the only damage you could do to the bronzes.

This sort of vandalism is a scourge of our age and country. No Italian would think of vandalising a work of art, ancient or modern. Indeed, the world pays immense sums to visit the art and architecture of Italy. Fountains are sacred there. Here they are littered with beer cans and nobody thinks of building them any longer. Many fountains built by the Victorians have gone dry because of vandalism. When Peter Nicholas installed a superb fountain at St David's College at Lampeter, students threw detergent into it to induce foam, and then gradually destroyed it bit by bit. It had to be dismantled. The little towns of Bavaria and the Tyrol nearly all have a central feature, a fountain or statue which the people treasure. It is all too infrequent in British life and iconoclasm has often been endorsed as official policy. Most of the mediaeval glass in Canterbury Cathedral was personally attacked and smashed by the Dean of the time in a fit of iconoclastic zeal. Hardly any statues of the Madonna and Child survive. British iconoclasm and philistinism is a sad fact that artists know too well and dread. There is something in the collective British soul that denies art. Yet history shows that a nation's art is its treasure, its heritage, its palpable message to future generations of how it was at the time the artefact was created.

Cilfach Syr O.M. Edwards a Syr Ifan ab Owen Edwards

(The word *cilfach* translates as nook or arbour, but means rather more. It is also a place set aside for contemplation or discussion.)

David Jones and the
Vernacular Tradition

Television is such a fleeting medium, and although these days it is possible to record and tape one's cherished moments and so accumulate a private archive (much as one has collected books over a lifetime and constantly refers to them in the way of professional research or simply for private delectation) I have the impression that TV, that is, video archives, will never take on the dimensions and certainly not the aura of a book library. Will we ever have to find a word, like 'bibliophile', for a collector of films or videos, in the sense that the activity can be taken as a contribution to scholarship, however small and private it may be? In my own modest library, in the fiction area alone, there are certain foundational books that I would not be without, which I would have to replace in the case of theft or loss of some sort, books like Joyce's *Ulysses*, Bely's great masterpiece *Petersburg*, or Italo Svevo's *Confessions of Zeno*, celebrating Dublin, Petersburg and Trieste respectively.

I cannot imagine any such core to a TV library or archive. I am too old, too firmly fixed in the Guthenberg Galaxy of the printed word, incapable even of understanding the new technology of knowledge. I should require my four-year-old grandson to guide me over the switches if ever I were to acquire a video. In the making of words on paper, I am dependent on pen or old-fashioned manual typewriter, not even an electric one (I tried one and it ran away with me like a bolting horse). As for what is called a word processor . . . no, it is too much to ask me to read from a TV screen. I actually *love* print on paper.

This may all sound like some unendearing personal eccentricity, but I make no apology for it. It is not only my age, but the way I am made. Yet I might stretch the imagination and nominate one or two films that might form my core archive, like the old black-and-white *Monitor* films. I remember one by John Berger, trying desperately to explain the sculptor Giacometti. I recall Berger saying something like: "But why are they so thin?" as he stood amidst a group of Giacometti's stick-like people.

Berger talked as brilliantly as usual, yet he never really explained *why* the sculptures were so thin. There is always this difficulty with art and explaining it verbally. Yet critics constantly try, and I see nothing intrinsically wrong with trying if it helps lead some people towards rapport with art. But as a non-scholar, and therefore like most people, I dislike the activity when a critic embarks on a sort of internal language, blinding us with science.

Yet I can appreciate the difficulties, and since one of our distinguishing features is curiosity, people do like to know, and sometimes resort to critics for enlightenment. So the critic tries, and in trying finds himself tying knots from which he cannot extricate his prose. I am about to do this. For, confronted by a collection of David Jones's inscriptions at an exhibition, I found myself trying to explain to myself their particular appeal. First, *did* they appeal, or was I guilty of some rather precious 'pseud' worship? No, I was convinced, without argument, that these artefacts did indeed appeal very much to me. I coveted them. But why?

Having all my working life made a partial living by inscribing decent lettering on stone, the first thing to be said about David Jones's inscriptions is that, by classical standards, they are *bad* lettering. Brought up in the same stable as David in the Eric Gill Workshops, I have even tried my hand at bad lettering, as relief from the discipline of good lettering, which can be an awful strain if followed non-stop over a long period.

So, let us first admit that we are talking about '*bad*' lettering here. It would take a book to trace the traditions of '*good*' lettering, beginning with fine Roman inscriptions like that on the Trajan Column in Rome, probably the most graceful of all (and grace is one of the attributes of classical lettering, just as of an Ionic column), through the manuscript forms of the Mediaeval Church (the Book of Kells comes to mind at once), to fine printing like that of Aldus Manutius the Venetian, to the present private presses like Gregynog.

Where does David Jones stand in all this, he who has been such an exemplar in reminding us of our traditions? What interested David was the 'sub-Roman' or vernacular tradition that went alongside the great classical inscriptions. I have one in my possession, a simple little *titulus militaris* from the second century commemorating one Theophilus Barbius, soldier of the cohorts. It is rude, yet owing something in its spacing and proportion of letter to letter and line to line, to the great anonymous masters of classical Rome. The execution is poor, as though by an amateur within a tradition but without the equipment to sustain it. These sub-Roman scripts are prevalent all over the Roman Empire, and especially in the outer provinces like Britain. There are examples in the National Museum of Wales, in Chester, in Segontium at Caernarfon, at Caerleon, and even in a few remote churches and sites way out in the remoter landscape.

David Jones was aware of these, of course. That much is evident in his work. He was also aware of the classical canon exemplified in the Trajan Column inscription which was such a model for all subsequent inscriptions. David learned all of this while staying with Eric Gill at Capel-y-Ffin and at Pigotts in Buckinghamshire. When I myself went to work at the Gill workshops, in my bedroom at Mary Gill's house there was a little boxwood carving, Byzantine in feeling, on the chest of drawers. It was a Madonna and Child by David, and Mary told me I was in David's former bedroom. Gill was dead by now and David had settled finally in Harrow on the last reclusive spell in his life. The little carving was a fugitive thing, delicate in execution, as intensely private as David in all his ways. I never

Welsh Arts Council

David Jones

met him, fearing to intrude on that privacy. He eschewed public life and depended on a few devoted friends: Harman Grisewood, Valerie Wynne-Williams, René Hague and Douglas Cleverdon. In carving that little boxwood block, David had followed Gill in the habit of making relief sculptures of used or rejected blocks. But there the resemblance ended, for although David owed a tremendous debt to Gill and his Tertiary Dominican life at Capel-y-Ffin and at one stage was engaged to Gill's daughter Petra, they were inimical in their attitudes and practice in art.

Already, when David carved this little Madonna, he had adopted the inimitable lettering style which we recognise and love when we see it on rare occasions at an exhibition or in some private collection.

This rough, vernacular sort of lettering, the mark of some individual craftsman or artist rather than of some school or workshop, is frequent in Wales. Occasionally I take rubbings or photographs. One dated 1780 in the churchyard at Llanfair-Harlech has an endearing lower case Roman. The difference between David Jones and the anonymous Llanfair craftsman is that David *knew* better, but chose not to practise. Or was it that he *could* not? I am sure that, had he applied himself, he could have cut the classical, disciplined Roman of Gill. Gill the master would have been very insistent on it. But remembering the shattered nervous state after his war experiences (the tissue of his masterpiece *In Parenthesis*), David probably knew it was not for him. I know of no classical inscription, either cut in stone or painted on paper, by David Jones. But his researches in two areas, the Latinity of Rome and the Romano-Celtic folk culture of Britain, and their interaction, influenced both his writings and his painted inscriptions. They are inextricably complementary.

But why? Why are the inscriptions so appropriate to his writings? Is it that the writings are so fractured, so heavily referential as to be discontinuous? Is it the conflict of the metropolitan classicism and the peripheral vernacular? Of innocence and experience?

I have already covered this in the essay 'Not Built but Truly Born'. The further you are from Rome, the heart, the thinner the pulse as you get out to the extreme limbs of the Roman Empire, like Wales. So, although we have classical Roman inscriptions in Wales, they are already vernacular, a debased classicism. When the native Celt tries his hand, it is at once imperfect *and* appropriate. We *expect* them to be imperfect, as though perfection would be both inappropriate and pretentious. The native hand is rude, expressive of his station as member of a subject race. This would not be conscious, as with David Jones, but natural to a man who was subject to the influences of Rome but debarred from its wealth and power. That, in a way, has been the condition of Wales through the ages, even when it was a Celtic heartland, since internecine strife is a Celtic malady that works for any invader. It is a Welsh condition, the obverse mark of empire and economic hegemony. It is that peripheral feeling. It is David Jones territory, a place with Roman soldiers manning wild outlandish stations on the edge of Empire, far more cut off in Wales than in the relatively comfortable barracks on Hadrian's Wall, for Wales was never settled in quite that way.

> From the fora
> to the forests.
> Out from *gens Romulum*
> into the *Weal*-kin
> *dinas*-man gone *aethwlad*
> *cives* gone wold-men
> from *Lindum* to London
> bridges broken down.
>
> (*In Parenthesis*)

The native Celts seem never to have submitted as the Romans would require, though there is much Latin in Welsh. With this half-settled Roman status there is the vernacular imperfection of style that exactly reflects it.

So David Jones paints a Roman letter without the classical disciplines and constraints of the metropolitan models. There is a wildness and freedom, a refusal to conform, that reflects exactly the condition of those outposts of Empire in a world of deep and defiant vernacular consciousness and tradition. In David Jones, it is not only the letter forms, but their kind, for he often introduces lower case among capital letters, or Celtic script or uncial among Roman characters.

But why? I have tried to explain what I think, but, as with all great art, I have failed. Yet I am curious, conscious as I am of my own training and practice in 'good' Roman lettering and having made a living at it. I know how strong and appealing is that sub-Roman of David Jones and his models like the little *titulus militaris*, carved little more than a hundred years after the death of Christ. The disciplined, traditional characters I have carved over the years are no more than you will see anywhere where there is a care for these things. But the sub-Roman is a reflection of the condition of Wales. "From about the age of six", David Jones wrote in *Fragments of an attempted autobiographical writing*, "I felt I belonged to my father's people and their land, though brought up in an entirely English atmosphere." I know the feeling very well, the pull, the magnetism. Perhaps this feeling alone demands that odd vernacular or sub-Roman David adopted as his style, so inimitably his own.

Take the exquisite painted inscription in the Welsh Arts Council collection *Cara Wallia derelicta*. A Gill inscription would be formal, to order for a client, an artefact of grace and refinement, within the classical constraints of the Trajan Column inscription. The David Jones inscription, by contrast, shows a refusal to conform. His alignment is out, his individual letter-forms are freely vernacular and inconsistent, he mixes Roman and uncial, he disposes his colour arbitrarily. In short, he breaks *all* the rules. Yet every inch of their apparently perverse style is calculated. The inscriptions were important to David personally. He used them as 'cards' (like the Mass cards on the altar) to help him through his daily office as a Tertiary Dominican. In their origin, these inscriptions are no more merely aesthetic objects than was an Italian Primitive 'Annunciation'. Like it, they were 'utile' (a favourite DJ word), things to be *used* in daily life. So they had to be just right, and this vernacular is right and proper to their purpose.

His complex mind saw a sort of European stream of consciousness. He loved his Welsh ancestry, but chose rarely to visit Wales, perhaps fearing either to test his unsure command of vernacular Welsh, or to lose his 'Roman' connection.

Does this help explain David Jones's inscriptions? I doubt it. They need neither explanation nor apology. They simply *are*. Perhaps the only thing to say is that, like many of his paintings with their inner references, they are paintings, simply that, and that the 'signs', as in a Mark Tobey 'abstract', can be read according to your whim or your capacity. But of their *rightness* I have no doubts whatsoever. But still, that does not explain them.

Cara Wallia Derelicta, by David Jones

Sensation

Sculpture's basic concern is palpability, sensation. It must appeal or reach out to our sense of touch before it can work. One looks at sculpture, but for impact it is our sense of touch and of presence, not just our eye, that is involved. "Before it can work . . . ?" Well, sculpture may have much more to say after or while the initial touch is made, but unless that impact is made first it can hardly say it.

Take Gianlorenzo Bernini's work. The fantastic rococo felicity of his *St Teresa* in Sta. Maria della Vittoria in Rome is what appeals to us first. In blank terms, a woman in billowing drapes floats on a cloud, in blissful expectation of the dart from a young angel standing erect diagonally left above her. It is so very palpable, such audacious carving of marble, so billowing, soft and white, a veritable cloud cushion of marble, that we might come away with only that memory. We cannot physically touch it, it is sited beyond our reach, but our sense of touch responds to it at once. The work literally occupies space in a way to invite our sense of touch. But then messages abound, ecstasy, mystical union, and, to our post-Freudian minds, there are obvious sexual intimations throughout — that erect androgynous angel, those parted lips. But first and foremost, Bernini knew the *touch* of marble.

And this is where our own appreciation of sculpture lags behind painting, for our sense of touch is weak compared with that of sight. It is not just touching as a conscious act, but that sense of touch which involves both touching and passive response to the artefact or to its nearness, as in the case of the *St Teresa*. A bat flies by its sense of touch through a sort of radar mechanism and it touches nothing in its flight by exercising this sense. Our sense of touch, by comparison, is partly atrophied by the physical security of civilised existence. We no longer require our sense of touch for hunting or for securing our defences, and we no longer need to *make* so many things, they are made for us by machine and robots. Ours might be dubbed the Age of

Reproduction, for even as we confront some great art work, building or landscape, we reach for our cameras — click, click — and we turn to the next sensation, anxious to record and reproduce our immediate response before we have had time to drink it in.

I have the feeling that impatience with the circumscriptions of over-civilisation has been a factor in driving many painters away from drawing-room canvases, either by using enormous wall-size grounds or by extending into three dimensions. There is a concern for palpability as much as for illusion, so that a nether area of sculpture/painting now occupies the stage as much as the traditional polarities of painting and sculpture. It is a need to invoke the sense of touch as well as of sight.

Most sculptors have experienced slight irritation at the state of a work returned from an exhibition. One part of it may have been touched and polished by the rub of countless fingers. I have one green-patinated bronze head on a public site within reach and the nose is now highly polished down the right side. The site was not of my choosing and the subject now looks like a tippler. But it is all a compliment, I suppose, that the thing invites touch, even if only to feel what it is made of. St Peter's bronze foot in the basilica in Rome is very highly polished by the devout kisses of the faithful.

So sculpture and its definitive concern with palpability seems very much a basic part of human nature, however atrophied and however ill-understood. It is very diverting to read various Renaissance minds trying desperately to define the nature of sculpture and its difference from painting. It is quite obvious it disturbed and puzzled them, and we have to remember that behind them they had the centuries of Byzantine iconoclasm which forbade the making of images in the round. Benvenuto Cellini was not content with a two-dimensional, description — "A piece of sculpture is begun from one point of view, then it is turned little by little so that, with the greatest exertion, a hundred views of it and more are made." Any sculptor knows that is clutching at straws. It is not made or conceived like that at all, but how to explain it to the layman? Henry VIII's codpiece to his armour in the Tower of London has been worn loose and polished by the rubbing of countless women in the past. A Cockney fertility rite?

Sculpture's concern with the sense of touch is quite dis-interested, not concerned with utility but often allied with it. The Willendorf 'Venus' is a very palpable object, so is a Cycladic

Doll, and so is Matisse's monumental series *Le Dos* in the Tate Gallery. But the touch of the little 'Venus', for instance, means far less to us than it did to the man or woman, priest or soothsayer who once rubbed its bulbous forms in some fertility rite. We do not function like that any longer, now that our sense of touch is relatively weak. It is no coincidence that Matisse is the most sensuous of painters and I find something very palpable about his paintings. *Le Dos* is not the work of a painter running out of steam, but rather of one bursting with it.

Sculpture will always bear the primeval burden of touch, of a physical presence antithetical to our own, not illusory but *there*. It will delight, move or disturb us more through this primeval, half-atrophied sense and that is why it is never quite so consoling or reassuring as painting, why it is the darker sister of the two. There are always more painters than sculptors, and if demand is any guide, paintings are bought more readily than sculpture. Sometimes I wonder if sculptors are not less understood and therefore less acceptable to society, though I accept this could be pure nonsense, a sort of professional paranoia. Sculptor Michelangelo once met painter Raphael on the streets of Rome. "You look like a prince with your court" he said. "And you", replied Raphael, "look like a hangman with your henchmen." Looking back, it was a very odd public vendetta against Epstein in the twenties. His *Rima* is a very mild affair, yet it was painted, tarred and feathered regularly, as though to exorcise an evil spirit.

In the high Renaissance there was a certain tension between the two disciplines and Leonardo was particularly outspoken on sculptors and sculpture in his notebooks. "A very mechanical exercise causing much perspiration which mingling with the grit turns into mud. His face is pasted and smeared all over with marble powder, making him look like a baker, and he is covered with minute chips as if emerging from a snow-storm, and his dwelling is dirty and filled with dust and chips of stone . . . " and goes on to describe the more gracious life of the painter — "well-dressed . . . his home is clean . . . often enjoys the accompaniment of music", all unhindered by the interference of "hammering and other noises". These were the words of a man whose greatest sculptural project had failed with considerable loss of face, a great equestrian statue for Ludovico Sforza that never got beyond plaster and finally crumbled to dust. They were also the words of a tidy, fastidious man who saw his greatest rival Michelangelo as a man who flung himself into a rough bed in his dusty clothes with five others and must have smelled to high heaven. Leonardo was possibly the most civilised man ever. By the same standards that cannot be said of Michelangelo, who bore within him the primeval burden of carving out his palpable presences, as though externalising his agony. But it may be that he plumbs greater psychological depths, and certainly the most casual acquaintance with the great 'Captives' in the Accademia in Florence reveals disturbing powers that Leonardo did not realise.

Sculpture's specific quality, its palpable presence, is also its incubus. Of course, paintings have sometimes assumed a similar palpable presence and Berenson spent a lifetime exploring what he called the 'tactile values' of Florentine painting. It is a matter of transcending the limitations of two dimensions, of 'coming out' at us. Sculpture on the other hand *is*, it impinges physically. This 'objectness' is a real problem. It may be too like our own corporeality for comfort, it is 'pushing', it shares our own airspace. The twelfth century Scandinavian chess men which are always on display at the British Museum are an example. When these tiny figures were cast up in a chest on the coast of the Isle of Lewis in 1831, the crofter who found them on raising the lid fled for his life. We may be more sophisticated, our sense of the numinous may have been stunted since the Industrial Revolution, and our sense of touch blurred from softer living, but it is still there and we do actually seek to touch sculpture and respond to it with the aboriginal instinct of the cave-dweller. We may think we have gone a long way, but I believe we are just round the corner from the people of the Willendorf Venus. We still invoke, propitiate and reassuringly touch.

The Ludovisi Throne

I had talked too much in praise of sculpture at a student seminar. "Any questions?" A student asked me which piece of sculpture from the past I coveted most. I played a bit for time, being rather stunned by the question, though it was meant playfully enough, a typical student ploy to puncture an old hand's plummy enthusiasm. We discussed terms of reference etc, but finally agreed on the simple criterion, which one would I like to live with all my days. Various distinctions were important, of course, such as historic provenance, even a definition of sculpture, but in the end we agreed we knew what we meant by the question. An answer was required, that was all.

"No doubts, at all," I replied with all the uncertainty of a pseudo-master of history and taste — "The Ludovisi relief in the Museum of the Diocletian Baths in Rome." None of the students present had heard of it and there was a general air of disappointment. Furthermore the college library could supply neither illustration nor slide to demonstrate my point. Was I not stalling, when there was the whole world to choose from? Well, perhaps, yet the more I thought of it, the more I liked my rather arbitrary choice.

First the 'thing' itself is a doubtful object, a four-square rather self-contained presence that is somehow very likeable before you know anything about it or have taken it in. Is it a throne? Of all the chairs, thrones, stools that one comes across (and in Wales Eisteddfodic chairs loom large), it is unique. There is nothing quite like it. As usual, having considered it for years as a throne, the scholars think it either a sarcophagus and even the remains of a monumental bed carved in marble by Polycletus for the Heraeum at Argos. Its only rival then for monumental intention would be the great slate bed made for Lord Penrhyn and still shown off in Penrhyn Castle. The Ludovisi Throne looks ancient and ceremonial, yet also strangely new and fresh and approachable. Even without decoration it would be a sculptor's piece in its candid blockiness. Typical Greek stelae (or indeed

The Ludovisi Throne. The front panel (56 × 42 inches), originally thought to date from c. 460 B.C.

the frieze from the Parthenon) explain its low carving technique. There's nothing much to it, but the assembly of parts is rare if not unique. In a joiner's sense it is nicely made. There is something deeply satisfying about this throne or sarcophagus or bed-head as object. The relief itself, so the scholars tell us, depicts Hera at her bath in the spring of Canathus, attended by two nymphs. It is simply beautiful.

Now the Greeks were uninhibited about nudity, but neither had they any illusions about it. We were just learning to live with nudity again after a century of prudery, and now we have made such a cliché of it in the gutter press that we could lose it again. There is more draped work from Greece than full nude, and the most popular, she of Melos, is half-draped, possibly the most fetching mode of all. But she is a great hockey girl, a centre-half compared with the slip of a girl on the Ludovisi relief, Momma compared with Lolita. Is this unfair? Of course it is — but I was asked for my favourite, and show me the man without Lolita proclivities — inside every law-abiding male citizen there lurks a Humbert crying to get out. Anyway, Hera rises before our eyes, as though borne of the water, and this gentleness of movement is assisted by the upheld draperies, performing a graceful arc across the whole panel. The drapery is evanescent, clinging intimately to Hera's maidenly form, so that her small pointed breasts are suggested with the utmost delicacy. This was a trick first played by the Greeks, who knew its appeal, its essential sexuality. They played it over and over again, from those archaic girls from the Temple of Aphaea on the island of Aegina, to the late Venus of Melos and the great winged Nike of Samothrace in the Louvre, but never so fetchingly as in this little icon of emerging womanhood. My motives may be suspect, but I shall not protest too much. Hera is the most touching homage to burgeoning beauty, her icon is pure love.

I have always thought of Hera as matronly wife to the errant Zeus. If indeed this be Hera, then she is little more than a maid, a Susanna half-concealed from the elders by her nymphs' tender ministrations. She is most delicately sketched in — she wears a sort of tight chemise, or *chiton*, clinging intimately to her figure as she emerges from her bath. She is exquisitely poised this side of prudery, still observant of the Latin quality of *pudor*. In fact, except for the suggestion of the folds of her shift round her neck, she might be nude to the navel. It is sensual, yet pure. Her face is side-turned to the nymph on her right, her hair waves with that crimped regularity that was so popular in our *quattrocento* ladies and is coming back today in some of our own nymphettes. A hairband keeps it under control.

The composition is symmetrical, yet not quite. There is a satisfying complexity within its essential simplicity. The nymph on Hera's right shows both feet beneath the hem of her *chiton* and Polycletus has disposed the two limbs and the drapes, an awkward problem in relief, with touching inaccuracy. He had all the true artist's faith in the suspension of disbelief.

Looking back, my choice was rather obvious, a personal choice from among any number of like character. The Hera belongs to what was called sentimentally 'The Golden Age', but not without reason. Everything was speculative, tentative, open. A memory of practically any product from the earlier Egyptian civilisation will illustrate what I mean. There, posture was stiff and hieratic, whereas the Hera is free and moving. I might have grandly chosen the great charioteer of Delphi, because his movement off one foot away from the stiffness of the earlier *kouroi*, his departure from uncompromising frontality, was symbolic of what was happening to the human spirit. Hera confirms this freedom. From images like her and the life that engendered her stems what is free and open and simply good in human nature. Yet it is left implicit, never overstated. Hera is a fine blend of thought, feeling and making, an icon of an age and a people. She disposes us to dwell on the good and to transcend evil.

To have chosen a Greek subject was perhaps too obvious for the students. The art of our century has been marked by many alternative views to our western heritage — primitive, African, Aztec, Asian, a whole world is now open to us. But in the end I still believe in Occidental Man, however much he may have betrayed his animating spirit. And I have no doubts where that spirit first breathed. We may struggle to grasp the convoluted ingatheredness of the Oriental spirit, we may need to know something of it to counteract our own thrusting extraversion. But in the end, we need only read Thucydides to recognise the mark of Occidental Man that is us, the sly cut and thrust of debate, the insights into human nature, and the whole rag-bag of aspiration and failure that is too recognisably us. And there is a reassurance about this. Hera, by example, is still with us, on the King's Road, on any campus, she is what we have begotten, and what will beget those who follow us, loving us and rejecting us.

All I know is that, when I first saw her in the Terme Museum in Rome, she quite took my breath away.

P.S. As I have suggested, scholars have argued over the Ludovisi Throne and have come up with different theories. The latest is that it is a nineteenth century fake. My response to that, as with the provenance of the Turin Shroud, is: 'So what?'

Blessed Delinquent

In my advice to students to contemplate keeping some form of diary alongside their sketchbook, I stress its private nature, its potential as a source of ideas for work. I stress also that ideas are private, only to be published as work. When a psychiatrist, intrigued by the sexual undertones in Henry Moore's work, suggested to the sculptor that he might care to be analysed, Moore rightly refused, preferring to keep his obsessions to himself, locked away from verbal probing. 'Keep your obsessions to yourself' might be good advice to all artists. Talking them out is one of those 'enemies of promise' so ably described by that arch-victim, Cyril Connolly.

Yet, at my age, and unlikely to make many more carvings, it might be of interest to disclose one small obsession of mine. It is not from some hidden recess of the mind, like Moore's rounded and holed forms, but rather a literary obsession, something engaged by the 'forebrain', as Lawrence Durrell would describe it. I refer to the Biblical figure of Jacob.

An obsession, if that is what it is, a haunting, a preoccupation, a filling of the mind at various periods of life, must have a beginning, a planting of the seed. I am pretty certain Jacob first sat beside me in Sunday School, when as a child of five or six I would have it told to me as one of the earliest Bible stories beloved of teachers in religious instruction. It is not in the least boring, in fact, as 'soap opera', has one of the best plots going. Jacob occupies several chapters in the Book of Genesis. It is more than enough to set the mind pondering, and Thomas Mann pondered at great length in his beautiful, worldly-wise *Joseph and his Brethren*.

The main thrust of the story is the conflict, not of good and evil (which is also a good plot always) but of earthly fallibility and divine infallibility. Taking the Quakerly concept that there is "that of God in every man", Jacob is a prime example. Yet he is tainted with all that is fallible. How could a man who founded a dynasty, who was in touch with God, and who is revered in the

Biblical memory of Jew, Christian and Moslem alike, how could such a man be *so* duplicitous?

So the idea of Jacob sits with me (the very word 'obsess' is built up from the Latin *sedeo*, 'I sit') and I have carved images of him throughout life, as though to externalise or exorcise something. Perhaps it *is* a personal need, some urge from the literary forebrain to reconcile the conflicting demands of sculpture and writing. I would not care to examine it too closely, but prefer to accept and get on with it, with being obsessed and creating something out of the obsession.

And the carving of such images is also part of a private mission that probably has no future, namely, that we might consider sometimes returning to 'narrative' sculpture, so beloved throughout the ages, from the Parthenon frieze to the Stations of the Cross in any Catholic Church.

The narrative of Jacob is primordial. Old Isaac, at the age of forty, worried about his wife Rebecca's barrenness, entreats the Lord . . . "and the Lord was intreated of him" . . . (this passive voice is typical of the King James Bible, which I quote throughout for its language). The Lord is slow to deliver, for Isaac was threescore years when at last Rebecca conceived. It was twins and how they fought within Rebecca. She too went to the Lord, patiently enquiring, never "entreating", as men will, why this conflict within her womb.

> Two nations are in thy womb
> And two manner of people shall be separated from thy bowels,
>   sings the Lord,
> And the one people shall be stronger than the other people;
> And the elder shall serve the younger.

There is no doubt, trouble lies ahead. Poor Rebecca, to mother such a pair. But it is the Lord's will. Henceforth it is the younger who shall command her help at every stage in life's journey. The first child came out red, "all over like a hairy garment", and was called Esau. The second, Jacob, caught Esau's heel on the way out and in the original Hebrew this is of some significance, lost in the English or the Welsh, for Jacob is "of the heel". Esau grew up a hunter, while Jacob was "a plain man dwelling in tents". This, in view of the subsequent story, I would dispute.

The first duplicity occurs when Esau returns worn out from the hunt and finds Jacob busy over a mess of potage. "And Jacob

sod potage", it says — (there is not only duplicity here but, as
Dylan put it, "using language"). Esau breezes in, flushed from
the chase, a carcass over his shoulder I have no doubt. He is
famished, smells the appetising air of Jacob's sodding potage
and asks for a portion. Jacob seizes the chance to bargain. Esau
shall have this lentil soup if he will sell his birthright to Jacob.
Esau, the careless man of the hunt, readily agrees, "tomorrow I
might be dead and that soup smells good, man" being his
philosophy. "What the hell", you can hear him say. But it is
crucial to the plot, it will come up again.

To be absolutely fair to Jacob, Esau is a bore, with nothing
much to say for himself. Having sold his birthright for a mess of
potage, we must assume he was such a healthy extravert that
such values implicit in the blessing weren't worth a fig to him.
Freud was not the first to divide the human race into the two
very convenient compartments of introvert and extravert. Like
male and female, there are shades, but Jacob and Esau are
extremes. In fact Esau can do nothing right. He even marries
outside the tribe, "which were a grief of mind to Isaac and
Rebecca".

Then, as Isaac grows old and blind, he charges Esau the elder
to go hunt venison and to bring him some "savoury meat".
Rebecca, convinced that this is a sign that Isaac is about to pass
on the blessing, suborns her younger son, he who shall be served
by the elder according to the Lord's will. She orders him quickly
to get some venison and cook it while Esau is out in the wild
hunting his quarry. She clothes Jacob's neck and hands with
goatskins and decks him out in Esau's raiment. Then Jacob goes
into his blind father, who is at once suspicious, wondering, as
well he might, how Esau has arrived so quickly from the chase.
In answer to his father's query Jacob answers "I am Esau thy
firstborn". Time and again Isaac is incredulous, but Jacob
persists. Finally, as Isaac bends down to kiss his son, he smells
Esau's raiment with the healthy scents of the field upon it: "See,
the smell of my son is as the smell of a field which the Lord hath
blessed: Therefore God give thee of the dew of heaven, and the
fatness of the earth, and plenty of corn and wine: Let people
serve thee, and nations bow down to thee: cursed be every one
that curseth thee, and blessed be he that blesseth thee". It is
done, the blessing has gone to the second-born, it is irredeem-
able, not to be abrogated, however deceitfully gained.

When Esau returns, Isaac can only say " . . . by thy sword
shalt thou live, and shalt serve thy brother". Esau, enraged,

vows to kill his brother. Rebecca takes Jacob aside and warns him, adjures him to flee to her brother Laban in far Pandanaram. On the journey Jacob sleeps by the wayside, making himself a pillow of stones, and dreams of the famous ladder, with angels ascending and descending. Mariners, with their unerring instinct for a good yarn, have adopted the term 'Jacob's Ladder' for a rope ladder with wooden rungs which can easily be stowed aboard when not in use. Jacob dreams of the Lord blessing him yet again. This blessing must be sure, one feels, perhaps because of his duplicity in cheating Esau over his birthright in the first place. But the Lord has spoken, He will not go back. Jacob is the blessed one and Jacob, on waking, knows this is the Lord's place, Bethel, a name much loved in Wales and seen on many a chapel.

On he tramps with his staff, which is also remembered as Jacob's Rod by surveyors. He reaches a well where the people 'of the East' are about to water their flocks. Jacob asks if they know of one Laban. Sure enough they do, and point out that Rachel, daughter of Laban, is about to arrive with Laban's flock. So Jacob meets Rachel, is guided to Laban, and finds there another daughter, Leah. "Leah was tender-eyed, but Rachel was beautiful and well-favoured." A bargain is struck: if Jacob serves Laban seven years, he shall have Rachel. But there is deceit yet again, for after the seven years are fulfilled, it is Leah whom Laban sends in to Jacob. Jacob is furious when he discovers in the morning that it is Leah and not his beloved Rachel. "It must not be so done in our country" Laban replies, "to give the younger before the firstborn. Fulfil her week, and we will give thee this also for the service which thou shalt serve with me yet another seven years". So Jacob has two wives and another seven years service. The Lord once again must have had a hand in all this. "And when the Lord saw that Leah was hated, he opened her womb: but Rachel was barren." Leah bears son after son, Reuben, Simeon, Levi, and then Judah. Rachel's jealousy knows no bounds. She turns on Jacob, who deflects her anger by declaring that it is the Lord who has withheld, not he. Rachel is determined, however, and sends in her maid Bilhah to Jacob. "Behold my maid Bilhah, go in unto her; and she shall bear upon my knees, that I may also have children by her". Thus Dan is born, ostensibly of Rachel; and yet a second time the ruse works and Naphtali is born.

Leah, in turn envious of this late child-bearing by Rachel, sends in *her* maid Zilpah to Jacob. "And Zilpah Leah's maid bare Jacob a son. And Leah said, A troop cometh: and she called

Bethel (1983). The sculpture was destroyed in 1988 by a falling tree.

his name Gad." There are many etymological goings-on here in
the Hebrew, each name denoting something significant. A
second son is born to Zilpah and is called Asher.

Follows a family quarrel between Leah, Rachel and Jacob,
over a field of mandrakes, which only followers of *Dallas* might
understand if you substitute Oil for Mandrakes. The outcome is
that Jacob must sleep with Leah, so late in the day, and she bears
Issachar, and yet again, Zebulun, followed by a daughter,
Dinah. Leah feels at last that she has measured up to the
requirements of a woman, in Jacob's eyes at any rate, and most
certainly before Rachel, "because I have borne him six sons".
Rachel takes up the burden once again and bears Joseph, around
whom, with his many-coloured coat, hangs many another tale.
Jacob has had enough and beseeches Laban to release him. They
bargain on what might be called Jacob's redundancy payment.
Jacob shall remove from Laban's flock all the speckled ones, as
his due.

This provides another chance for Jacob to exercise his guile.
Perhaps the only way to describe this peculiar episode is to quote
direct from the King James version if only to see the lengths to
which Jacob stooped to deceive:

> And Jacob took him rods of green poplar, and of the hazel and
> chestnut tree; and pilled white strakes in them, and made the white
> appear which was in the rods. And he set the rods which he had pilled
> before the flocks in the gutters in the watering troughs when the
> flocks came to drink, that they should conceive when they came to
> drink. And the flocks conceived before the rods, and brought forth
> cattle ring-straked, speckled, and spotted. And Jacob did separate
> the lambs, and set the faces of the flocks towards the ring-straked,
> and all the brown in the flock of Laban; and he put his own flocks by
> themselves and put them not unto Laban's cattle. And it came to
> pass, whensoever the stronger cattle did conceive, that Jacob laid the
> rods before the eyes of the cattle in the gutters, that they might
> conceive among the rods. But when the cattle were feeble, he put
> them not in: so the feebler were Laban's and the stronger Jacob's.

I am not sure if I fully understand this ruse, but I take it to
mean some sort of auto-suggestive selective breeding in Jacob's
favour. And now I understand why surveyors called their rod a
'Jacob's rod', for is it not a "white-straked rod"?

Now Laban's sons, incensed at this vast increase in Jacob's
wealth at their father's expense, fly at Jacob. Jacob is quite up to
this, waits on the Lord, and preaches to Laban's sons on the

importance of the Lord's blessing to him, and why that implies that he shall enjoy this increase in wealth as of right. He then flees before they can come to their senses, as well he might.

It is the gospel of determinism over free will. However disgracefully Jacob behaves, the Lord is with him, and there is nothing the sons can do to harm him. Even Rachel, in a moment of deceit, takes her father's household images as they flee. When Laban chases the fugitives and catches up with them at Mount Gilead, he searches furiously among Jacob's tents. He cannot find his images anywhere. In fact Rachel is sitting on them and will not move. "And she said to her father, Let it not displease my lord that I cannot rise up before thee; for the custom of women is upon me."

Eventually Jacob and Laban make a treaty before a pile of stones on which both swear. Laban returns to Pandanaram, and Jacob sends scouts ahead to search out his brother Esau's feelings about his return. When he hears that Esau has set out to meet him with four hundred men, Jacob is so afraid he sends further scouts, each with a flock as present to buy off Esau. It is then that Jacob, alone, fights with that strange assailant during the night — "and there wrestled a man with him until the breaking of the day". Jacob's thighbone is dislocated in this struggle with the angel at Peniel.

And so the story proceeds, on and on, like some Biblical soap opera, for it is far from over. There is yet the story of Dinah's defilement by the son of Hamor, Shechem. This is an awful episode, for the bargain for Shechem to make Dinah an honest woman is that Shechem and all the males of his tribe shall be circumcised. This they promise, but while they are still sore and immobilised, Jacob's sons fall upon them and kill them.

Let us have no more — it is *too* Biblical and horrible on occasion. The quarrelling is endless, yet there is also a sort of blessedness too. It is the human condition. However much we may think we have conquered the universe, we are still subject to something above and beyond us, fate, providence, destiny, God, what you will. Jacob is the archetype. Those sons of his, heads of the twelve tribes of Israel — is there no end to their squabbling? The story of Joseph alone is worth volumes, witness the Mann saga.

Then there are psychological types in Jacob's story. What was the bond between Jacob and his mother Rebecca? What sibling jealousy divided the twins? What ruses would Laban's daughters Leah and Rachel go to to bear Jacob sons? To what lengths

Jacob and the Angel (red sandstone boulder, 1952)

would Jacob go to increase his wealth at Laban's expense? Yet he is blessed of the Lord, he carries the blessing within him, to hand on, however deceitfully received in the first place. The Lord deigns to communicate direct with Jacob, he is the Chosen One. Is this not the dread concept of predestination? James Hogg's terrifying work *The Diary of a Justified Sinner*, in which the hero can commit any crime whatsoever yet go unpunished because he is justified, is the tale of one blessed of the Lord. It is a form of dread fundamentalism, based on determinism, that one part of the human race is blessed, the other damned whatever good it may do.

And yet, and yet, it is a story that has attracted artists, Rembrandt and Gauguin supremely. Gauguin's version of the wrestling with the angel is most touching, all laid in a Breton setting, the high-coifed women gazing on, as though coming out of church with the vision from a sermon still upon them.

In all the departments of human frailty, except perhaps undue modesty, Jacob is expert. He is liar, even to his blind father. He is adulterer several times over, though not without the collusion of his two wives. He is a fraud and a cheat, going to great lengths to deprive his benefactor Laban of his wealth. Yet he is blessed of the Lord. If ever there were need to demonstrate the childish dictum 'it's not fair', Jacob's story is the one. Perhaps that is why it struck home in Sunday School.

And so, from time to time, I carve an image of Jacob, if only to get something out of my system. I am by nature a lapsed agnostic, finding it supremely difficult to believe, yet impressed by the numinous, by the immanence of something . . . something I possibly find in Jacob, the deceiver, the wrestler with angels, the blesser of stones and pillars, the archetypal flawed nature blessed nevertheless by the Lord.

There is a further ingredient to this Jacob obsession. Whenever I visit Bryn Cader Faner on the slopes of Ardudwy, I think of Jacob the raiser and blesser of stones and columns. It is probable that, but for language (Jacob's was probably Aramaic, forerunner of the classical Hebrew that is spoken in Israel today), Jacob would have recognised his outlandish Celtic brethren in the small business of rearing flocks on stony hillsides. It has to be remembered that Celts lived not too distant from Jacob country, in Galatia in Asia Minor, and Celtic tribes would be contiguous with Semitic ones in that corner where Asia Minor fades into the Levant.

I recall that just as I was about to leave the Army, at the age of twenty-seven, an older colleague who was a writer declared that I was old enough to read Thomas Mann's *Magic Mountain* with benefit. He was right. Had I read it earlier, I should have missed the essentials. I have already in this book recommended Mann, and I cannot leave the story of Jacob without recommending *Joseph and his Brethren* as one of the century's great master-pieces. But let it not be too early, for there are lessons in life that are lost on the young, just as there are some to which the old have become too blind, like poor old Isaac.

The Voyage Out from Innocence

People talk of having 'a good war'. I have never fully understood this, though I take it to mean survival after lots of action and 'fun' on the way. There is no such thing as 'a good war'. Like my father I entered my war innocent and came out experienced. By this I mean that for the working class there was little of that 'experience' that we gather accrued to those with access to Oxbridge, Bloomsbury, the Apostles and all that. We travelled no great distance from the family hearth. A bicycle was treasured as extending one's orbit beyond ten miles or so. Nor did life seem worthy of record. Beyond a figure like W.H. Davies, there were no working class poets, though a few painters and sculptors managed to break out of the bounds of class, especially in the Midlands, where Birmingham and Wolverhampton fostered an artisan class based on industry and the crafts. One or two of my generation even graduated to the British School at Rome, an immense step before the war.

Like my father, as I grew up I was regarded as a suitable candidate for a Letts diary in my Christmas stocking, and like him I was conscientious for a week or two then lapsed or lost the thing. This is a pity, for much of my youth is lost in a limbo — that place, according to the Oxford Dictionary, "in which forgotten or unwanted things collect".

Again, like my father, any war records are lost, though I recall keeping a diary in Europe. Since most of military life is hanging about, packing and unpacking, with short bursts of action (especially true of a parachute unit), it is no wonder that a pocket diary disappears. But I notice that, when we embarked for a longer voyage to the Middle East at the end of hostilities in Europe, I felt constrained to buy a notebook and there recorded that first long voyage from home. I was twenty-six years old, perhaps mature enough to value, and evaluate, the experience. Certainly, reading it now through the ravages of damp and mould, I realise I was little more expansive than my father, bless his memory, with his "sailed from Mudros 8 a.m. for Alexandria.

Slept under tables". Dammit, he was actually sailing over Homer's wine-dark sea, past islands of immemorial beauty and legend. How was he to know? Was I any better? Perhaps a little, if only less brief. My notebook for 1945 does summon up for me a remembrance of an ordinary lad's first long sea voyage. Nowadays mere babes in arms fly by jet to the Mediterranean, and football 'fans' are quite as likely to turn up in Mexico as in Chelsea.

★ ★ ★

Saturday 22nd September 1945. 02.00 Reveille. 04.00 march past Devon Guards (Bless 'em all) and saw last of Carter Barracks [Salisbury Plain]. Southampton 06.00. Embarked *Dunnotar Castle.* Crowded accommodation in hold forward. Boys throwing last letters and coins to doubtful characters on quay. Frantic girl (or wife) with father (or in-law) looking for *him* — joy all round and cheers when found near stern. Balloons(?) [perhaps I wasn't as innocent as I seem to remember!]

Sunday 23rd Sept. Raised anchor in stormy weather. Hugged coast in increasingly rough seas. [Follows a passage in which I obviously fail to cope with mal-de-mer.]

Tuesday 25 September. Sunrise over Cap Finisterre, lying low and rugged on horizon. Silver shafts of light breaking on sea. Calmer — everybody in good spirits again. No more land till dark, when light off Lisbon appeared. Reading Ruskin *Sesame and Lilies.*

Wednesday 26 Sept. C. St Vincent. Breakers on cliff faintly visible. Dolphins, whales spouting, porpoise, gannets. Straits of Gibraltar ahead.

Thursday 27 September. Cool breeze from East — choppy. Wonderful range of mountains on Spanish mainland. Afternoon Atlas mountains. Floodlit scene at night on deck — figures in green, white and red vests bent over housey-housey cards, like a host at worship.

Friday 28 September. Atlas mountains behind Algiers, high and steep out of sea, with rugged sky-line, reminiscent of Cozens. Reading Henry James *The Europeans.* Skyline of windblown vegetation, perhaps umbrella pine.

Saturday 29 September. Pantellaria on Port beam. From sea looks like a dream island, in shape anyway, rising gently out of the sea to the north and gradually to a peak in the south. Southern edge steep craggy cliffs, showing pale marks of wartime shelling. Hospital ship on port beam. Very hot and in the afternoon we had a boxing contest. There are some strange characters among the crew — a little wizened man who does nothing but peel potatoes and vegetables. I notice he rolls his own cigarettes, in spite of the mess of his hands. Tonight he seemed in ecstatic mood, peeling dry parsnips. In the galley, an Irish cook who ladles out the food. He rapidly gauges the meat ration for 18 men. Always clean and white despite the heat, he is dripping with sweat, which he deftly wipes off every few minutes with a dish towel he keeps round his neck. Big, handsome, efficient, bearing a burden of intolerably hot work without the perpetual groan of army cooks.

Sunday 30 September. Very hot. Clocks on half-hour. Sea very blue — one can imagine the hand, dipped into it, would emerge dripping blue. A swallow has dodged the column and is voyaging at ease with us. No land visible. Reading Balzac *Le Colonel Chabert* — "Do you know, my dear fellow", Derville went on after a pause, "there are in modern society three men who can never think well of the world — the priest, the doctor, and the man of law? And they wear black robes, perhaps because they are in mourning for every virtue and every illusion".

Monday 1st October 1945. We run into a rain storm. A great belt of dark blue cloud ahead of us. Little deck rivers search us out and we flee for better shelter. Rain beats the sea's surface to an undulating oily skin, and creates the illusion of mist in each trough. No glisten and sparkle now, but a vast opaque expanse, with the horizon interrupted by falling sheets. Hot clammy stillness in the air, no breath of air, and you sweat for no apparent reason.

But in the afternoon the sun shines from a sky broken with fleecy cloud.

Am I right in thinking our tempers are already shorter? I think so. We are so crushed together there is no release, no means of being alone to work it off. The noise at meals, the loud-hailer and the inevitable mix-up of belongings all contribute to nerves.

On 'D' Deck today there was truly a spectacle. There wasn't a single vantage point the swallow could find, the place was so covered with tanned bodies. The only open space was the *sanctum sanctorum*, the boxing ring, where the 9th Batt. were to fight the 3rd. The latter in red vests, the 9th in white. The ship's Sergeant-major presided on one side of the ring, the referee on the other, for he keeps out of the ring in Army boxing and calls fouls, holding etc., from outside. That is why the crowd must keep quiet. Three 3-minute rounds and they were mostly good sport, as far as I could judge. At the end of each round, the crowd heaved a sigh of relief, chattered, roared, then hushed as the referee signed for silence. A little red or green flag was raised at the end of the fight, to declare the winner.

Tuesday 2nd October 1945. After breakfast we see a warship moving fast along the skyline, signalling to us. Nobody could read morse. We sail at half speed all day, expecting to see land any time.

Wednesday 3rd October 1945. Off Haifa at breakfast. Low hills rising out of the sea with town built on slopes. Long range of Mount Carmel. Mist rising from hollows. Disembarked by big flat bottomed barges. Many schooners and cargo vessels in harbour, one Italian destroyer, barges, ketches and the usual Arab bum-boats.

* * *

The discovery of this worn-out old notebook certainly brings back that voyage. The first mention of Mount Carmel touches me, because later I was to become very much acquainted with it, there making many friends at No 1 Army Formation College, an educational establishment for undergraduates in the ranks about to be demobilised. There they were given a month's course of Liberal Studies to ease their return to academic life. And there I met the girl who was to become my wife. Courtship was clandestine. Judith Maro was recently demobilised from our own ATS, but as far as our army was concerned she thereby reverted at once to the hostile native Jewish population, since we were implementing our League of Nations Mandate, standing neutral between Arab and Jew and loathed by both officially. Judith and I were married in great secrecy at a charming private ceremony by the District Commissioner, Mr Lowe, who exercised the correct discretion that it was none of the Army's business and did not inform them. When I returned after Lunch to camp a married man and announced to the Commandant that I had married that day, he was astounded. "Who to, for God's sake?" he asked. "To Judith", I replied cheerfully, and his reaction was a prompt handshake and a libation, for Judith had indeed been a most popular member of our college community and nothing could have been as artificial as the non-fraternisation ban we were supposed to exercise towards those who had only yesterday been colleagues and friends in our own forces. Among the Staff at the College were Michael Stewart, later a foreign secretary in a Labour Government, Willie Hamilton the ardent Republican, and Huw Wheldon. The Commandant was an amiable academic, Allan Champion. None of us saw any reason to give up friendships we had forged with the local people, whether Jew or Arab.

But the Holocaust was not far behind us. Many of us had witnessed in Europe those pathetic columns trailing out of the labour and concentration camps. As for the Jews themselves, they were determined that nothing should prevent them establishing their own homeland in Palestine. The seeds of the present Middle East crisis were sown then, if not earlier. The British stood in the middle and it was an unenviable task. When, in 1948, we decided to withdraw and leave the Jews and Arabs to fight it out between themselves, there was immense relief in Britain, and especially among the evacuating forces. By then I had been demobilised.

There is then a great gap in my 'recorded life'. There was home to find, work to establish, family to rear, none of them easy tasks just after the war. All I can find of any record is something I wrote when I reached the ripe old age of fifty when, apparently, I felt the first intimations of going downhill. Well, by now fifty reads in my mind more as the end of youth! But the section that is preserved seems to me more what a journal should be about and I wish I had made more of it at other periods of my life. It is only in advanced age that I preach to students the value of diary or journal or written notebook.

The section has survived only because, when I was asked to contribute to a North Wales magazine called *Mabon* (alas, now defunct) I simply handed over the passage I had written around my fiftieth birthday and called it 'Quinquagenarian'.

Quinquagenarian

In the summer of 1968, when the Italian middleweight boxer Nino Benvenuti won the World Championship, he had the temerity to do so in the USA. That meant two things: first, he cocked a snook at the new world from the old, and second, he did it, as far as the citizenry of Rome was concerned, at five in the morning. All night, up to and beyond the decisive hour, the traffic in Rome kept circling, transistor sets blaring, and when the final verdict was broadcast the drivers tooted their klaxons in one great mad, celebratory cacophony. An old widow, lonely, racked by a painful illness, committed suicide, leaving behind a note: "There is nothing more to live for. Benvenuti has become champion. I die. Adio!". The Italians have always possessed this capacity for immediacy in their living and their dying. It follows from the untranslatable *carpe diem* of the ancient Romans.

I want to relate this ephemeral quality of daily living, this immediacy, to the putative permanence of art. I say 'putative' because art is permanent more by reputation than in reality. More art has of necessity and quite properly died than has survived. The physical quality of permanence, like happiness in life, is incidental, fortuitous. Two of the most enduring of media, bronze and ceramic, were used for their intrinsic quality as pliable and sympathetic materials rather than for some vague yearning for immortality. If so much Greek art has survived, it is chiefly for two reasons: first, its requisite strength as building material, for that is what objects like the Elgin marbles are; and secondly, the ever-increasing regard it has enjoyed through the ages. Both these qualities are extraneous to the objects as the embodiment of art and immortality. They are cherished now either as museum pieces or as adornments to the material life of the surviving rich. They have become a sort of super currency.

Now this view of permanence rather sours the art scene at the moment. Today we have, more than ever before, a divisive element in art. We see the rapid metabolic rate of change, schools wrapped up in a decade of fashion quite as likely to be forgotten the next. We even have a candid recognition of this in the art schools and a conscious trend towards impermanence and immediacy. At Leicester recently I watched with fascination the researches of a girl student into rice-paper sculpture. Above all, we witness a terrible divorce from the past. This cool rejection of the values of the ship-owners of this world, who buy impressionist paintings to adorn their yachts, is in my opinion wholly commendable. But alas, my capacities do not match my sentiments. Like some miscreant, I return to stone as to some well-beloved mistress, her through whom I saw long ago, whose every ploy I know, whose clinging permanence I spurn. Why must she be so importunate — I keep returning to her and I cannot help myself, she and I are so inextricably and mal-adjustedly linked together for life. I return from each loving fray covered with dust, knuckles scarred, grit in my navel, to pick up the rice-paper with civilised fastidiousness in an attempt to re-orientate my disordered occidental life. But it is no use — and anyway, I have my friends, survivors in the chancy life-permanence race, bits from the world of Archaic Greece, Cycladic dolls, turtleshell omoplates from the Santa Cruz Islands, Luristan bronzes that were meant for no more than adorning a horse, whale-bone plaques from 9th century Norway, Muslim Stelae, standing stones from our own hills (supremely Bryn Cader Faner in Meirionnydd), all objects from the hands of navvies like myself, better navvies mostly, but often much the same, navvies ineluctably tied to the trade in hard durable materials that scar them for life and may have nothing to do with a view to permanence, and may or may not appeal to Mr Onassis. In the end I not only submit to the doubtful pressures of permanence, but I gladly acknowledge a debt, a gratitude to the past, not merely to the things men made, but to the way of life they led, to their manipulations of material and landscape to a given end.

* * *

Take just one instance among many. Why, I wonder, have men from the earliest times raised winged or horned presences in their chosen environment? There must be some reason. It is not merely the one consummate image from Samothrace which now stands defiantly captive at the top of the staircase in the Louvre. The theme is there all the time in one form or another, a perennial ideogram, and even today I see students raising fibreglass winged or horned eminences in the crowded art-rooms. I have an idea that somewhere within we have always confused the horned and the winged image — the former presenting threat, menace, insecurity, death and destruction, power against our vulnerable selves — the latter, visually often similar in profile, offering flight, release, embrace, power over others, victory and angelic beatification. I find the Horns of Consecration that the Minoans raised on the South wall of Knossos against the landscape equivocal in effect, threatening yet placatory, symbolic of our inner division — *ego et id*. It is even there in the most serene of creations, the Ludovisi Throne now in the Diocletian Baths in Rome. But here the civilising effect of city life in Classical Greece has transformed the threat of the upward held drapery into prophetic love, benediction so to speak. And yet the throne echoes the Minoan horned image in some ways — the tension of straight and curved.

Man's pathetic attempt to contain the threat of the horns and aspire to wings mark much of his image making. Even that strange Apocalyptic image *mulier amicta sole*, 'a woman clothed in the sun', puts that celestial mystery, the moon, beneath her feet, *et luna sub pedibus eius*. It is no wonder that Christian artists have never ceased to grasp this beatific image in windows and statues depicting the Virgin.

Was it symbolic and prophetic of man's perpetual division that the questionable aims of the Crusaders were finally thwarted at that crucial battle in the Galilee, the Horns of Chittim? The very name has always summed up for me the most tragic conclusion to an exercise in unwonted material ambition underpinned with mystic faith.

If I were asked for my chief concern in sculpture, I would say, therefore, that this sort of imagery, integral or peripheral to human activity, consoling and disturbing, is my concern. When I live, or, what medium I use, exercise me less than this immemorial 'ideation' in sculpture. Today, certain schools of sculpture emerge strongly, and the current cool concern with 'objectiveness' is only partly my concern, it is only incidental to it. Therefore I must be content with unfashionableness.

★ ★ ★

Miraculous, the flight of measured thought
Crosses the rebel fire of burning youth;
A choir of tranquil heads

Moving sublime
Through Raphael's heaven, from distance into time,
Inspired the pupil Perigino taught
To paint heaven's periods,
His mind being in its silence fixed on truth:
Unrest in calm, calm in unrest he sought.

(from Vernon Watkins' 'The turning of the stars'.)

In the end, despite public statements, a sculptor reaches the state of the last two lines — or if I'm wrong to generalise, this is what I feel about it and see in a master like Brancusi. This state is implicit in the work progression of most sculptors, from the overstatement, elaboration and emotive overtones of youth to the implosive simplicity and serenity of his years over the hill.

It is implicit too in that religious ambience of great works, however secular their content, so that we read these lines alike in the Rondanini Pieta as in certain images of the American-Japanese sculptor Noguchi. In neither case is it the content that breaks down our potential opposition, it is that "silence fixed on truth: Unrest in calm, calm in unrest . . . " that reaches out and involves our troubled minds. "When we are no longer children, we are nearly dead", (Brancusi), and again the master — "Simplicity is not an aim in art — one attains simplicity in spite of oneself by getting near to the real sense of things".

Noguchi regards sculpture as an enduring antidote to the impermanence of so much current living. In the sudden balance of permanent/transient (and it *is* quite sudden, poised under the shadow of a mushroom cloud) I suppose I come down inevitably on the side of the permanent, if only by choice of medium. So much that is transient is created under the threat of the 'horned' image. My 'Nike' be it horned or winged, is hesitant, soft-centred, poised between threat and love, and if it disturbs as well as consoles, then my position is clear, or should I say unclear? That is why I love the poem 'Nike who hesitates' by the Polish poet, Zbigniew Herbert.

* * *

Trying somehow, and in desperation, to strike a spark in a group of rather recalcitrant students at a seaside resort, I recounted how I had emerged in the evening from the hotel on to the broad esplanade. I was merely going from the door to a

waiting car, across a wide pavement. But in that brief moment I
looked up at the sky. The light was dying out of it, it was quite
clear, and deep, deep empyreal liquid purity. Across it, with
deep intent and flying high and straight, and all in the same
direction, and somehow widely spaced across the whole extent in
random open formation, crows, scores of crows. It was the
height, the firm intent and the steady direction towards some
unseen destination, all against that deep empyrean, that moved
me. This was on the 13th September.

How strange that on the 18th, back at home, reading Giedion-
Welcker on Brancusi, I came across this: "Nothing describes the
work of Brancusi better than the vision of the great Brahmin
Rama Krishna. The legend goes that this transformation was
effected thus: 'One day in his 16th year, as he walked across the
fields, he raised his eyes and saw, very high in the sky, a flight of
white herons. The white livingness of the beating of wings
against the blue of the sky, the simple *rapport* of the two tones,
eternally inexpressible, suddenly pierced his soul. That alone
and nothing else. Nothing more was needed. Something snapped
in him, something new emerged. He fell as though dead. When
he raised himself up, he was no longer the same man. He brought
to human kind a message of sublime purity . . . '."

I daresay a flight of herons would have more significance than
crows. Be it remembered however that the saying *"Duw a
ddarpar i'r brain"* "God looks after the crows" belongs to
Anglesey.

★ ★ ★

When people question my allegiance to Christianity, sug-
gesting that in 'this day and age' it could be a curb to creativity in
some way, I can only reply that they are wide of the mark. If my
work fails in any way it is simply in terms as a good or bad artist,
and not as a Christian or agnostic artist. If as a man I seek God
and desire to worship him, I believe that in no way impairs what
creative imagination I may possess. In the sense that for me faith
and belief add a dimension to life, or rather that unbelief would
diminish my life, my Christian faith, vestigial though it be, is
essential to me. That part of it, the glad acceptance of the fourth
dimension is a consolation whose lack would disturb me. I would
have to *fight* unbelief, indeed for many years I did fight it. It is
part of the dimension too that great areas of human suffering
disturb me so deeply that I want to cry out "Lama, lama?",

"Why, Why?" But within the acceptance of that dimension I simply work, no more, no less. And the adverb 'simply' is calculated, for it is from the simple basis of a working life that I live and love — and of course there is nothing very extraordinary about that. It is what most people would claim, not least artists of serious intent. "Art is that way of work in which man uses his free will" — and my acceptance of the fourth dimension enhances my free will. Non-acceptance for me would impair it, would set up alien tensions within. My love of family, home, men, work and landscape must be acted out in the divine ambience of the fourth dimension. But I have no illusions that it is all as unfashionable as my pathetic allegiance to stone and cast metal. Yet it is a compass reading, a guiding star, a course to keep, or to lose.

★ ★ ★

There is a little verbal image of Paul Klee, *symboles consolateurs*, that I find immensely satisfying. No critic or historian has ever really 'nailed' art. It defies it. Far be it for a journeyman like me to try. I can only admit to a feeling akin to Klee's verbal image when I am busy with some image of my own. And while I confess to no burning desire to communicate, I believe the hope is always there that others contemplating and living with the image will find it *un symbole consolateur*. Just as Brancusi once said "Things are not difficult to make; that which is difficult is to put ourselves in a state of making them", so I hope the beholder will share this 'state of grace' that has gone into the making of the image.

One writes ideally! How rough life is however, even here at the edge of the western sea, immured from seething Europe by mountains. Although I may seek that sort of perfection of the poem in each work I approach, I fail, of course, yet I hope there is poetry in the trying. All the time, beneath the "intolerable neural itch" of the trying is the gnawing recognition of the virtue of silence. Vernon Watkins, divine victim of the Muse, writing in tribute to the other victim Dylan Thomas, had this to say:

> That was the centre of the world,
> That was the hub of time.
> The complex vision faded now,
> The simple grew sublime.
> There seemed no other stair

For wondering feet to climb.
"My immortality," he said,
"Now matters to my soul
Less than the deaths of others".

Yes, I know, one needs to know, and if my silence would
improve the lot of anybody then I would lay down mallet and
chisel today. It is, as Vernon so aptly puts into Dylan's mouth,
simply recognising that one's immortality, one's permanence,
matters less than a great deal that is happening to the human
race. This is not to stop, not necessarily to elect silence. But not
to be ready to, if it helped, would involve the death of the artist.
Art is, if you like, the efflorescence of this divine tension between
life and death, and if we remember that to a chemist efflorescence
can denote a turning to dust upon exposure to the air, then we
begin to get even nearer to the truth, and to understand some of
the current querulousness of youth. Quite a few artists of my
own acquaintance could very well echo the poor Italian woman's
note. "There is nothing more to live for" would become "There
is nothing more to say. Adio!" God knows I understand, and if I
work out my simple ideas in quasi-permanent media, nevertheless
I recognise that we pass like crows across the deep empyrean and
are gone.

Gregynog Journal

In 1981 I was honoured to be invited by the University of Wales to be its Gregynog Arts Fellow for the academic year. It was such an enjoyable experience that I found my sketch books of that period filled with words describing various meetings, events, experiences and table talk.

* * *

Gregynog, October 1981

One is aware at once of the fine stand of timber, the redwoods in particular, and in any weather. October was as wet as I remember. But nothing, not all the sodden remnants of a very wet month could diminish the imperial assertiveness of these redwoods, high-peaked, with descending flared skirts of hard green foliage. But more than that — the wetness has encouraged every kind of fungus, several vast plates flaring out of old tree stumps. On the well-tailored lawns, strident toadstools, glistening rather evilly after each downpour, flourishing rapidly to a dull scarlet fullness, then collapsing sideways in the morning with their own top-heaviness and lying like drunken dragoons in the field.

Met up with English section of Yr Academi Gymraeg. Met Harri P.J. in the grounds. He had nearly died of loneliness overnight, he said. Together we visited Francis Hewlett's *Hand*. It looked really colossal under a redwood, but a bit hidden away. I'd like to see it rising out of the middle of that great sunken lawn in front of the hall, but gardeners hate such interruptions to their lawn mowings. They have developed a genius for backing lawn-mowers into sculpture where they take umbrage.

When work (or is it business?) keeps you travelling too much, you actually miss out on life itself. It's not as though you got on horseback like Rowlandson or Giraldus and met everybody on the way. You motor or train frantically to appointments like

GREGYNOG. but is aware at once of the fine stand of timber, the hardwoods in particular, and in any weather. I took up my year's Fellowship October 5, 1981 and it was as wet as I remember. But nothing, not all the sodden remnants of a very wet October country weekend could diminish the imperial assertiveness of the redwoods, high peaked, with descending flared skirts of hard green foliage. But more than that — the wetness had encouraged every kind of fungus, several vast chanterelles in particular flaring out of old tree stumps. Then on the well-tailored lawns, strident traditools, glistening rather civilly after each downpour, flourishing rapidly to a dull scarlet fullness, then collapsing sideways in the morning with their own topheaviness and lying like a drunken army in the field. And all week they have flourished, the toadstools with an abandon that saw purpose in sheer quantity and number, a sort of fungoid cash flow or liquidity, coming and going:

the chanterelle more slow, more purposeful, bent on achieving a sort of structure, the great slabs exactly displayed to extract the most from the wayward light of showery days.

They have lasted, I notice, perhaps a little the worse for all the rain escaping. In an odd sort of way, their fissured corrugated surfaces remind me of the Burren in County Clare in Ireland, a limestone area of a distinctness that is rare

The Gregynog Journal: opening page (1981)

Welsh Arts Council or art colleges and real work becomes a mere interval in parentheses. As for requests to lecture or whatever, Huw Wheldon advised me: "Have three categories only — money — piety — and No!"

It's only when you examine details very closely in the Book of Kells that you get the true spirit of it. Scholars like Françoise Henry mull over it, of course, in a scholarly way — but I'm talking of visual detail, the strokes and terminals of letters, especially the ornamental capitals and some of the borders. There's one in particular, a row of seated men, large heads with punk hair-dos, no torsos to speak of, arms and legs shooting straight out from the neck and shoulders, forming a mad interlacing strapwork, so that each chap holds the leg of the previous chap in the air. The scribe must have been the monastic joker. One group could be taken as a coxed rowing four, four facing ardently left and looking hard at the cox, who in turn can't look them in the eye. He looks down — steering a wild course, I wonder? Three of the crew have crazy curlicue beards which set off intertwining with feet and with themselves. I have drawn this crew on a horizontal bias, after a facsimile. But in the original they are vertical, at the beginning of the Book of St Luke. Both the sense and the humour come to light then — sense, because seen vertically with their attendant texts, each looped torso and long leg makes the letter Q to go with the smaller vi, making qui in that long boring passage "Qui fuit Isaac — Qui fuit Abraham . . ." all those begats to Christ's genealogy. The humour must have relieved the boredom of writing all those begats in the scriptorium. For after the 'crew', the Qs become more formal as letters, but equally felicitious in their form and colour, circles and lozenges and squares infilled with glorious pattern. You begin to wonder what those monks were up to. Those hair-dos — pure punk — and beards like dreadlocks — a hand grasping a thigh — another holding his partner's peruke (to coin a phrase). Some of the later imagery of Picasso in his still fecund dotage, with arms emanating from any part of the body and careering off all over the canvas, isn't half as mad as some of Kells imagery.

Received the Edinburgh Poussin catalogue, with my re-creation of Poussin's model stage well illustrated. Nice to be named in the same publication as Sir Anthony Blunt. No question, spy, mole, traitor or whatever he was or was purported to be or to have done, you can't stage a Poussin exhibition without recourse to his knowledge. He simply *is* the world authority. Beside this immense scholarship, the spying seems a small aberration, but I could be wrong.

Back at Tyddyn Heulyn. We live in two quite distinct territories. Here, mountain and estuary in *y gesail* of Cardigan Bay, sheltered from north and east, and deriving every benefit from the Gulf Stream — though we do get high winds here. But quite equable seasons. Once over Bwlch yr Oerddrws, conditions stretch out a bit. At Gregynog in the humpy hedge-girt hills of Montgomery, the temperature can plummet at night, and already we have seen the broad valley below the cottage white with hoar-frost — unknown at almost any time at T.H.

October 24th. Cold front. Mountain tops dusted with snow, down to Moel Hebog. On Yr Wyddfa, down to Aran. Moelwyn Mawr quite white, but Moelwyn Bach still shy of snow.

October 25th. Warmer, though still white on summits. Yet no sign of snow over the way in Ardudwy. Quite often this part of the world is clear, and yet when you climb a bit and look inland, the Arenigs are white-capped and arctic in aspect against a cold eastern sky. The little oak outside our house survives all the rigours of the climate, most of all the wind, to which it bends nicely. Its sturdy bole spirals up and away from the prevailing wind, and its crown is subtly shaped to present the least resistance. In so far as you can love a tree, I love this little native specimen.

Motored back into the black evening to lecture at Gregynog, to Social Administration students. Talked generally about the artist and society, not so much his necessity, as simply his presence and the way his work has reflected his society — the hieratic mode of Egypt, the archaic smile of the early Greek *kouroi*, the introspection of a Byzantine mosaic and the enlightenment of the Quattrocento and so on. Not a difficult thesis, but to laymen like these students, not a viewpoint that had occurred to them.

November 2nd. A lovely autumn day, all changing lights, the mountain flanks copper and verdigris, dead bracken and green pasture washed clean by all the October rains. Motored to Aberllefeni in morning to pick up Wakefield slate panel. The quarry is at the top of a side valley with a bluff right before you at its head. Aberllefeni village is a row or two of quarrymen's cottages, trim, well-kept, neighbourly. (Cliff Morgan's phrase — "the comfort of the terraces"). It was travelling up this valley and seeing a man breaking through one of these fences that gave me the beginnings of my sculpture 'The fence', bought by D.H.

at the Cambridge exhibition. Definitely autumn — clear, crisp, a chill in the air, leaves like a million pound-notes underfoot.

Talked to a Nigerian student over Lunch. He was dreading the coming winter, particularly snow. "I wouldn't say Cardiff was world famous for its precipitation", I comforted him.

"When does it start?" he asked. "January? February? I'm really dreading it."

"Sometimes it doesn't start at all." Clearly he didn't believe this. "And when it does, it may not last overnight," I continued. "If it's a bad winter, which isn't often, it may last a few days. Longer than that is phenomenal in Cardiff." But he was determined not to be convinced, and clung to his dread of what might never happen.

Met an old farm-hand, retired, who wanted to talk. I was sketching, or trying to. He had worked on Gregynog Home Farm. He wanted a bit of a grouse, I could tell.

"That must have been a privilege," I said.

"Well, no," he replied, rather sharply. "It wasn't all er . . . what d'you call it now? It wasn't all, you know what I mean . . . "

I tried to help. "Cakes and ale?" I ventured.

"Milk an' 'oney!" he declared, delighted to have found *le mot juste*. He went on to have a jolly good grouse about the bad old days. Accent distinctly west country, I thought.

" 'Twould 'a' been all right if you coulda gone straight to the fountain head, like," he said flicking a bent old thumb in the direction of the Hall. "But there was allus the manager, like, between you and them. They was right . . . ", and he paused to assess if swear words would be appropriate in my presence (after all, I was sketching Welsh/Hereford crosses and one was even a full Welsh Black).

" . . . they was right . . . " But I was not going to help him this time, being curious to see if he found the right word for his retrospective indignation . . . "right — er — sort of a bit of a blackguard, you might say, especially that . . . " I was disappointed.

"Bit of a bugger, was he?" I interposed for his benefit.

"Ay, now, there you have it, bit of a bugger, you might say . . . " and on and on he went with his beefing. The only way I was going to stop him was to admire his stick.

"Holly?" I asked. "No, not light enough colour."

"Na," he replied, again looking for the right word.

"Not blackthorn either," I went on.

"That's right," he replied, but clearly not satisfied, "bit of a thorn to it."

"Very nice, very nice indeed," I blathered on.

"Ah!" It had arrived. "Prunus!" he said with obvious relief. I was surprised that a good Latin name had lodged itself among the grumbles and rambles of his old country mind. We then mourned the passing of the old Welsh Black, horns and all, and parted, he satisfied with his grouse, I dissatisfied with my sketching.

November 20th. 'American Studies' Course came in last night and at once I sensed a liveliness. Even at breakfast this morning, three academics plunged ardently into a discussion on post New Deal labour relations. One American, one Scot (who had galley proofs of his forthcoming book with him), one Englishman. My second-class little mind stood off somewhat, protected by Alpen (I mean, you mustn't get the damned stuff *too* wet). But I noted that, like my old farm hand friend, they sometimes could not recall a name or title, and there were pauses, "er . . . you know what I mean", as of course they did, for a few seconds later out it would pop . . . "Tomlinson", or "Underwood". Now Bertie Russell, I recall, rarely hummed and hawed or stumbled. If he required a fact or a name and he knew it and needed to recall it, out it came, at once, crisp and renewed.

John Ormond rang from the BBC about Dylan's stone — terribly importunate, they want to "cut the film" of its making before I've even got the stone. "Ah well, we'll put it off a week or two etc". This all so that they can show the film on March 1st — Gwyl Dewi Sant. Nothing to be done about it. I don't exactly type those letters on stone. John queried the last line, thought the one line 'Time held me green and dying' did it all. But I replied I personally found 'Though I sang in my chains like the sea' very evocative, I saw weed washed by the sea and the tide, locked to the rock but singing in the whirls and eddies etc. I thought it a superb metaphor. John thought it was the line "that did the least work in the poem" (only a poet could put it like that). I said I respected his poet's opinion, but as a romantic I would fight for that line. "There you are then . . . " he replied, with that humility before a lay voice that it is so much John. And I? Anything but humble, arguing with a poet about a poet. But clearly John favoured discussion. And anyway, even a navvy like me should end his days able to say "I sang in my chains like the sea."

November 21st. Two US couples turned up, husbands on

sabbaticals. Charming, not in the least tedious. Jean Jones (one of the wives) wanted me to find out if there was a Jones crest. If there were, what would it be — an eagle (that being St John) with the motto 'Jones supra mundum'? At least something for the rest of the world 'to keep up with.' And come to think, those four words, in Latin, would be the most appropriate, as correctly generic, since all Joneses have to be lived up to. She bought a copy of *A Tree May Fall*. I showed her how to take a rubbing from a headstone, gave her a bit of heelball, and thin paper. She was so delighted she rushed out to their car and brought out a bottle of Riesling — 'Washington State 1980'. Well, it may not be up to Chateau Margaux '76, but we shall see.

November 22nd. We did and it wasn't!

Boxing Day. In temperatures around zero walked from Croesor to Llynnau Cerrig-y-Myllt and Llyn-yr-Arddu with Deborah and Tim Maby. Conditions only just bearable with glazed ice and an icy buffeting wind the worst enemies. The lakes frozen over, with a ripple of water over the surface here and there. The wind flurries over Llyn-yr-Arddu were thrilling, in a glint of shy sunlight. After a hard trudge through drifts and over ice we were glad to get home, change socks and feel warm again.

January 9th, 1982. By now we are so thoroughy immured from the world by snow that I was even out of touch with this sketchbook. While I was just managing, with the help of the gardeners, to get to the Tearoom where I'm dealing with the Dylan stone (it was too heavy to get up to the studio), the rest of my things are across the yard. Between them and me are 4-foot drifts of wind-blown snow. Yes, we are cut off. The world is outside, somewhere across the silence. We hear from it occasionally by wireless, TV and telephone. I am imprisoned with about 18 students and staff who should have gone home yesterday. One student walked down the drive, which has been partially cleared by the estate's own little tractor snowplough. He reported that 'outside', the only indication of a road was a level of snow 4 or 5 feet deep and even higher between what were evidently hedges. I recall that Nigerian with guilt!

It has been phenomenal. For two days and nights it has snowed, with a south-east to east wind blowing cruelly. Oddly enough, home and the 'western sea' has suffered just as much. Judith reports by telephone of not being able to get past the farm and Pete having to deliver his milk on foot. The whole country is crippled. For snow, it is as bad as 1947, though for just freezing and refusing to go away, 1963 will take a lot of beating.

January 10th. Perpetually sub-zero now. Of the outside world we hear only by wireless of towns and villages cut off, of impassable roads, cars abandoned, of warnings not to travel and to farmers that helicopters are only for extreme emergencies. When I finally got to the cottage this morning I found the loo frozen over and an icicle under the tap.

January 12th. My companions have decided to have a go at breaking out. Engines were gunned into action — then the police, by telephone, urged against it. About eight of them, in the end, decided to try by train, and were dropped at Newtown, after some difficulty, to await one of two trains all day. They are wise, I suppose. Tomorrow, just to help, the railwaymen are on strike! It's all like breaking a siege.

January 13th. This morning the Swansea lot got away at last. It was quite touching. At the porch as they were about to leave, I saw one lad holding hands with one of the little maids who look after us here. A week had been enough to forge a little friendship. They looked like a couple who had known one another some time and parted as though he were going to war. The normal 3-day extent of a course here is not enough to forge such a link and it must be very frustrating for the girls, to take a fancy to a lad then see him go after three days.

I have cut, somehow, 33 letters of Dylan. Not bad, considering. BBC filming has gone by the board, needless to say. And the Abbey are so tardy I can't wait any longer.

Talking of Westminster, irrelevently — a story I like about Asquith. An American, awfully glad to meet Asquith "after I heard President Wilson, Colonel House and your wife often talk about you". "What did my wife say?" was the prompt riposte. Another story picked up at table. Khruschev and Chou En Lai didn't get on and had a shouting match. "You're not a Communist. Look at me," says K, "I was born a peasant — you were born of the bourgeoisie." This took some swallowing. As farewells came at the airport Chou turned to K and said, for all to hear: "Well, we have one thing in common, you and I. We both betrayed our class!"

Or of Balfour, I like this: "I am more or less happy when being praised; not very uncomfortable when being abused, but I have moments of uneasiness when being explained."

January 17th. I finally broke out. The locality of Gregynog was reminiscent of Central Europe, which is used to this sort of thing. Local drivers were already getting used to it, charging their vehicles at slushy slopes, giving way good-naturedly, driving away through ruts and bumps and drifts of snow like any good Switzer.

February 12th. A Politics group in, about 70 from all colleges. This time they simulate a crisis, and in various groups they discuss, fulminate, negotiate and generally go on like real politicians — i.e. they eat and drink and talk well at regular intervals while the 'crisis' smoulders on. This time the 'crisis' is Poland. I note the Junior Common Room (which rather stinks) is labelled 'Vatican City State'. I must pop along to see what the nice comfortable Senior Common Room has become — my guess is 'White House'.

In the middle of this, Peter's letter on *Solidarnosc* arrives, with a ring of truth about it. He writes from Prague, so is nearer the seat of the affair than we are, and certainly than USA. Henry [Anglesey] thinks we're all wet, that the West has lost its nerve in the face of the domino theory. He points out that in terms of improving life of the people, by comparison with the West, Communism has been history's biggest failure. Who's to know? It depends where the respective countries started from. If the Tzar still ruled Russia, or the Emperor China, would things have been better? I very much doubt it. Yet queues in Warsaw, Prague, East Berlin, Bucarest; but not, I understand, Budapest at the moment. Is that a fair measure? After all, we had queues during the Cold War period. It depends not only on place but on time. We could soon slip back. Doris Lessing's *Memoirs of a Survivor* is darkly prophetic on this — civilisation certainly in its sophisticated perks, electricity in wires and water in pipes and sewage too — separates us from darkness and slime — only wires and pipes between us and chaos. What if they lapse for some reason beyond our control, if their source or their destination or their route fail us? We are too many ever again to cope with it as once did primitive man. So in that sense Communism *has* failed. In other senses too, in the pressure on the mind. So is the only alternative to be what-we-have-we-hold capitalism, even The Bomb, the ultimate banality and venality?

March 1st. Difficult to keep up with this book. Too much travel again, too little continuous work. Anyway, got to Abbey, where *y seremoni dadorchuddio* [the dedication ceremony] took place with due pomp and circumstance. Easily the best of it was Daniel Jones's music, which filled the hallowed and historic precincts with ease and majesty. Aeronwy carried it all off like a duchess, Caitlin not there of course. Son Colm from Australia was the spitting image but without the charm. One devotee in the file past afterwards reverently laid a bottle of Haig (beribboned) on the stone, which Colm patently coveted but which probably the Abbey beadles later filched. I trust it was cold Welsh tea if so.

March 11th. Another dislocated week. I must to London after Lunch, to record a *Did you see?* discussion at BBC with Susan Hill and David Butler.

March 16th. I attended a conference here on the possibility of a European Cultural Centre at Aberystwyth. Lots of cold water about — what is the matter with people? I spoke at last, out of impatience, which was cheeky of me, since it wasn't my conference.

March 29th. Read a lovely story of the Douglas-Home family, demonstrating the brevity not only of the British working class but of the aristocracy. Telephone announcing father's death — "William? Alec here. Home's dead." "Right. Thanks."

March 30th. A very cosmopolitan crowd in, chemists on something like 'the gaseous states of matter'. Very easy to talk to, all confident in their own field and ready to explore others'. So a Dutchman was very curious about stone-carving (he advises Dutch museums on conservation). A Dr Tamas of Budapest was wise about East-West politics, Dr Leibnitz shook her head over Israel when I asked her, and wanted to know rather about my own fellowship. The self assurance that goes with authority in a given subject is a marvellous catalyst to table-talk. How gauche and difficult an undergraduate group by contrast. There are some compensations for getting on in years. Not that all these eminent chemists are ancient. One or two look about 18, like our policemen.

March 31st. March gone already and still on inscriptions — maddening. I've lost even what notes I had on *Zorn*, which is a pity. I can't recall all that. What a loss to the world! After morning coffee, Dr Leach (one of the chemists) visited the studio. He is English, was evacuated to Ammanford during the war, lives now in Paris. We discussed the rewards of family life, how the preoccupations of artists and scientists seem to augur well for parenthood. We neither experienced much of what is called the 'generation gap' (a phrase invented as though they'd invented the thing itself, which is surely simply a biological fact of life to be taken aboard with the rest of life). We both enjoyed our children, all fledged by now, of course, and they still seem to enjoy us. A top chemist, he worshipped Henry James, and recommended that I sacrifice something, a painting or sculpture or whatever, to get and keep the Master's 3-volume Letters. I've no doubt — I'm absorbed in D.H. Lawrence's Letters. DHL to David Garnett on April 5, 1913: "You seem a bit sporadic, and one looks for 'the core of ardour'. If I were you, I'd be a plain dull person for a bit."

He could be speaking of Gregynog in another letter: " . . . and the pine woods are dark, with glittering flakes, and suddenly the naked, red-skinned limb of a pine tree throws itself into the heat, out of the shadow . . . ". But it's Bavaria.

April 8th. Continued reading DHL's letters, and started on Byron's. The former was mostly on how NOT to earn money by art; the latter from Cambridge on, is about how to take spending and debt to a fine art.

Easter Monday. By now the Falklands armada is somewhere in mid-Atlantic, Al Haig shuttles earnestly between London and Beunos Aires, and he and *esse signora* will probably earn a little bit of capital out of what began as an almighty political clanger. So goes politics. The only bit of honour I'd award to Lord Carrington, who took the blame and resigned graciously. A few top civil servants meantime will continue to earn their KCVOs and fat index-linked pensions, having slept awhile. "Two bald men fighting over a comb" says the great Borges.

April 22nd. Last night went to see the film of *The French Lieutenant's Woman.* I've had my doubts about Fowles all along, while enjoying him. The film was so very bad it increased my doubts. I was angry with myself too, for having been spoofed by all that publicity.

April 27th. The weather remains superb. After that winter it still seems hard to believe. As for the war, we've re-occupied the South Georgias, fortunately without bloodshed. USA in a panic, not knowing which side of the fence to come down on. And possibly another thing which I'm unwilling to admit — we're better at making war than they are. Not only our handling of the Iranian Embassy siege last year, but now, after an 8,000 mile voyage, we promptly and efficiently re-occupy the South Georgias. Probably an easy landing (no Normandy!) but it looks good in a world bemused by publicity. Whereas poor old USA could only bungle its attempted helicopter rescue of the Teheran hostages (a much, much more difficult, even stupid assignment) and failure makes dreadful publicity. It finished Carter, whereas Thatcher's poll is up 7%. After being nearly brought down three weeks ago, heads rolling left right and centre, she's now riding high. While intellectuals agonise, she knows the British working class's quick inclination to bellicosity if there's a hand laid on 'our kith and kin'.

April 27th. The Lady is going straight for the jugular, I think. Indeed, *The Times* reports we already have Marines on the Falklands (denied, of course — this is about nerves, and I must admit she won't be the one who is wanting). If we re-occupy the Falklands soon, she could win a general election with a large majority. That after being about to fall three weeks ago.

May 3rd. I'd better pack up as political commentator, and get on with my job. Nobody is going to win the Falklands, and we're all going to be poorer, not least those who will die unnecessarily over it. Had a cheeky letter this morning from Archbishop's House in Cardiff, requesting if I would like to offer a slate inscription to the Pope on his visit. I don't even support the whole razamattaz.

May 11th. Yesterday as I motored into Newtown, I saw a strenuous walker striving uphill out of town towards Tregynon, an old knapsack of carpet (a quintessential carpet-bagger?) on his back, in shirt-sleeve order. A hirsute, red young man in Hockney specs. Coming back, I was about to pass him — he'd gone quite a distance — so I stopped. "Where're you going?" I asked him — patronising motorist to sweaty hiker. "To Tregynon — and beyond" (I liked that — 'beyond' — Wales, UK, The World, The Universe, as we all wrote in our exercise books.) "Jump in," I replied right civily. Motorists are so condescending. "Thank you," he replied with the sweetest smile, "I'd rather walk if you don't mind." So off I drove, a little crumpled. Now there was a man after my own heart. But I was *in* a car and it's a dreadful disguise.

May 14th. Motored to Rhosgadfan to meet Norman Williams of NWAA. What a landscape. Seething with character. It has that primordial Celtic thing of being within sight of the sea and yet being secret and hidden away, up on a height that outsiders would be wary of approaching. Of course, beyond a bit of hill-farming (the little stone walls enclose fields not much bigger than those in Connemara), it was quarrying that made these settlements in the early 19th century. Kate Roberts lived here and wrote tales of it, its nobility, its petty squabbling and its innermost character. Two county planners met us on a disgraceful Council tip on Y Lôn Wen. Our brief, to devise some Manpower Services Commission scheme that would put a stop to dumping and to make a *cilfach* or something that would be worthy of the place and its great writer.

Bu'r olygfa hon
yn gyfrwng
i adnewyddu
ysbryd llawer
ac yn ysbrydoliaeth i
weithiau Kate Roberts
o Rosgadfan   1891-1985

This view
has refreshed
the spirit of many
and inspired
the writings of
Kate Roberts
of Rhosgadfan

Cilfach Kate Roberts: the inscription

May 21st. Last night the white mare dropped a foal, just below our cottage. By breakfast the long-legged prodigy was already finding his feet. By evening he was cantering like a Derby winner. Naomi writes from Israel, where she is filming, that it has rained solidly for three days! In May? Peter writes from Pilsen in Czechoslovakia, where he notices how the historic buildings are allowed to peel and crumble. Perhaps conservation of Baroque and Rococo is too expensive in the 20th century, especially in an economic system not based on conspicuous waste.

Once again that sepulchral MOD voice announced today: "Sadly, another of our helicopters . . . " Another dozen lives lost. It all feels like living on a huge overdraft in lives and *materiel*. Surely the Falklands War will appear in future history books as the most fatuous war ever. Both Argentine and UK subscribe.

May 22nd. Another letter from Peter. At his archives at last, after all sorts of Kafkaesque obstruction, prevarication and procrastination from the bureaucrats. He had visited K's grave, well-tended still, which is a comforting thought, considering that both he and his race are *non grata*.

June 8th. One of Glyn Tegai Hughes' [warden of Gregynog] beautiful fatuous tales: during the depths of the Depression, King George V called J.M. Thomas who was either Chancellor or Minister of the Colonies or something. Said King G: "Well, Thomas, how bad is the situation?" The reply was prompt: "Well, if I was you, I'd put the Colonies down in the name of the missus!"

July 20th. Went to Llanfyllin, having been reminded by a Radio 3 broadcast of the Brahms Clarinet Quintet by the Allegri Quartet that they were to play the Schubert Quintet this very evening at Llanfyllin, where Bruno Schrecker the cellist lives. Got there about 7, where the players were still sitting over a meal, and we plunged at once on the morality of the artist, between engagements or commissions, when nothing is coming in, signing on the dole. I confessed I had not ever, and didn't even know how to, or how one qualified. Nor did they. Yet they, illustrious and world-renowned as they are, also experience gaps, and nobody understands — mortgages, fuel, food bills, and rates etc., all the various outgoings continue while your income lapses for 2 or 4 or 6 weeks at a time. Anyway, no matter, we all confessed to valuing our freedom more than anything. And they played with such verve and attack that they brought the house down (or rather the church). The sombre and majestic Schubert was spell-binding. It is now half-after-midnight, a beautiful green moth has just flown in, and outside, that queer squeaky bird protests as usual when a light disturbs its sleep.

August 22nd. Edward Gibbon: "I darted a contemptuous look on the stately monuments of superstition." And after being overwhelmed by the great 40-foot dynamos at the World Exhibition in Paris in 1900, Henry Adams wrote: "All the steam in the world could not, like the Virgin, build Chartres." There are omissions in both statements, but . . .

September 6th. Isabella d'Este to Perugino on painting her portrait: "You are not to add anything of your own."

September 8th. Told the CEGB I was shocked their Dinorwig plaque bore no Welsh at all. Today I amended that. Tried my hand at a bit of *cerdd dafod* and wasn't far off. With the help of W. Beynon Davies, it turned out as: "O Lyn i Lyn, Goleuni', which was surely appropriate for a "pumped storage scheme". CEGB accepted it, anyway; not that they would know!

September 13th At my lecture last Saturday there was an Irish academic. I had rabbited on about the artist in society and at the end the I.a. got up and wound it all up nicely. He told the tale of getting on the train at Dun Laoghaire with poet Paddy Kavanagh in one corner of the carriage, another Dubliner in another corner. Paddy gets off at Sandymount. The stranger then asks I.a. who P.K. is. I.a. replies: "Ah, now that was Paddy Kavanagh the poet." Dubliner digests this, then says: "Ah, now, wouldn't I be knowin' 't was a poet the way he wiped his nose on the tail of his overcoat."

Sepember 16th. Impressions of Gregynog, now my fellowship draws to a close. The friendliness — I really meant it when I inscribed a plaque 'To G. with Love' to go under an azalea I'd presented. Trees I'd got to know individually. The Montgomery landscape, green and humpy with distant hills. The lovely little town of Montgomery itself, left behind by 'progress'. Then odd little things like that strange metallic thump in the night. I thought it was a fox turning out a refuse bin, but it seemed too regular and persistent. I learned it was the septic tank! I noticed it was more persistent when the hall was full. Then the local Hunt — only once or twice a year. Recently some cubbing. Hounds yelping and howling in the woods at dusk, and chaps buzzing up and down the drive in cars going at 60! The scent of blood, adrenalin flowing, all in a car?

But over all, the dreaming landscape and the friendly people, from the Warden down to the little kitchen maids.

I even managed to have a war during my fellowship. "Those bloated armaments which naturally involve states in financial embarrassments." (Disraeli in 1862, at a time when Bismarck was fulminating about his *Blut und Eisen*). Things haven't changed much.

Parasol and Blewit: from the Gregynog Journal (1981)

Second Wind

Dear Cary,

You ask how I came to write fiction. Since two novels, or rather three, are over and done with, printed, published, reviewed, presumably read or rejected, I am prepared to talk about them retrospectively, or rather, about their making, for that is how I came to be a writer of fiction. About any future plans in that vein I will not speak, rather as an actor will not talk of 'Macbeth'.

So — for it's always a very shaggy dog's tale — certain circumstances conjoin and I must explain them as briefly as I can. I was adviser in Fine Art Studies to the Ulster College in Belfast in 1968–71, and in consequence of this I was invited to examine and report on various matters further south, in Dublin, where the National College of Art and Design was in deep trouble, with a three-month-long student sit-in, causing endless embarrassment to Government and the Department of Education. I made certain drastic recommendations, which the College Board accepted, and they then asked me if I would care to implement them in person, in other words, to become the Director. For a self-employed artist more used to navvying on my own than to education in an institution, this was a drastic step, but I accepted the challenge provided they would agree to a short contract only, (in fact 3–5 years), would pay me a fee rather than a salary, and allow me to persist with my own workshop practice on a reduced scale. Thus I retained my freedom to return to the wild at my own choice and would not, so to speak, sacrifice my virginity.

In the event, the first year proved a political battle, and it took three hard years for things to shake down and my proposed reforms to take root. It proved a long war of attrition. I then warned the Board I would leave at the end of the fourth year, in order to give them ample time to find my successor.

In the meantime, I was nearly ill without my daily 'fix' of

creativity. I had to submit to being a politician and administrator. While there was a certain fulfilment in seeing my solutions and reforms taking shape, I was suffering the artist's withdrawal symptoms. Unable to actually *create*, draw, make sculpture, I was afflicted with an inward illness. This was the first circumstance to subscribe ultimately to the nascent novelist!

Quite early in this period of withdrawal from art-making, a member of my staff, Paddy McElroy the silversmith, sensed I was lonely and possibly unhappy. My wife was not yet able to join me, for family life is not easily re-adjusted to such urgent moves. Paddy invited me to take a drive with him over the Wicklow Hills one Sunday afternoon. He called promptly (not to be taken for granted in Ireland), we drove down Fitzwilliam Street, turned right into Mount Street, and as we crossed the Grand Canal, Paddy pointed out to me a rather ugly monument on the bridge, commemorating twelve Irish patriots who had fallen there while inflicting 236 casualties on a British Battalion trying to enter Dublin during the Easter Rising in 1916. This single tourist act, a Dubliner pointing out to me a memento of the Easter Rising, was the second circumstance to push me towards writing.

Paddy toured me round the hills south of Dublin. From one height it was so clear we could just see the distant heights of Wales peeping over the horizon, and I felt a deep *hiraeth*. Altogether it was a momentous day for the future scribbler, though I was not to know it at the time. During the ensuing week, the political in-fighting at the college became even more bitter and I was in the middle knocking heads together. It was depressing work at the time, though being an outsider helped me to maintain the right detachment. But the artist in me suffered appallingly. One night I went home very depressed, and suddenly the memory of those 236 casualties began to worry me. I looked up in my rather meagre library, found it was all too true, that a British Battalion had attacked Mount Street Bridge during the Easter Rising, and had been decimated before the dozen or so Irishmen were finally overcome.

The story moved me deeply for some reason, perhaps because the Irish side was commemorated while the 236 British casualties were an embarrassment, best forgotten. What must it have felt like to be on the British side in that brief engagement? One evening in the flat I began to write, just like that, as though writing a letter to a friend on an impulse. I am a compulsive letter-writer (just as I refuse to telephone, certainly over

business, especially when people ask me for a 'snap' estimate), so
there was no problem in stringing words together. I had no plan,
the words simply poured out spontaneously, page after page. I
found it exciting. It was not unlike getting on with a satisfying
stone-carving. I could hardly wait for the next evening.

When I got back to the flat next evening I read what I had
written. It was such unbelievable trash I threw it away in a fit of
self-disgust. Recalling that first attempt, I know that John
Wayne would have shown a certain interest in it as a possible
scenario for a script. It was awful — dying men piled up on the
bridge, their heels showing, rifles flung across the road as they
fell etc, etc. It was romantic nonsense. I was ashamed.

The political in-fighting at the college was at its most bitter
and life in the flat was depressing. Not creating made me feel ill.
Yet, having promised the College Board to solve its problems, I
was committed. I began to lead a double life, the outer life of the
politician and the inner life of imagining that Mount Street
battle. It continued to obsess me, and despite the disgust at my
first abortive attempt, I found myself one night returning to it.
The whole thing was at the back of my mind all the time. This
growing obsession was the third factor in setting me off as a
writer. I wrote and wrote, non-stop, into the night, knowing
from my practice as a sculptor that being an artist is first of all a
matter of actually *doing* something, drawing, carving, painting
or writing, and not asking any questions. This time I accumulated
18,000 words, and when I read them I recognised at once the
difference from the first lame attempt. It might not be very good,
but it had a ring of authenticity. I kept it this time. That first
evening's work eventually rested, almost untouched, somewhere
in the middle of the subsequent novel. The obsession remained
with me, would stay until I had invented, scribbled, revised and
assembled some 80,000 words.

I completed my political task at the college and despite the
knocking of heads together, the staff presented me with a
money-filled wallet on my departure. There are no half-
measures in the Irish — they don't *like* you, they either love or
hate you, and after the years of fighting, it was made clear they
loved me. It was a tremendous, not altogether sober send-off,
and it was a miracle that my wife and I eventually staggered
aboard the Holyhead ferry and said 'au revoir' to dear old
Ireland.

So, I had a wallet of ready cash, enough to see me back into my
old professional practice. My Irish secretary, who had typed my

scribblings at home for me, had seen that I packed the random manuscript. My wife encouraged me to tackle the pile of paper. The gift of a month or two's breathing space provided a fourth favourable circumstance for the nascent writer. This 'bursary' was an example of enlightened patronage in a way, an example of how a breathing space is necessary and might be provided for by an arts council or a foundation. I addressed myself to the manuscript with a clean conscience. As with the College, it was to be a limited contract, very limited indeed, but enough to see the job through.

Thus I became a writer. I had transcended the barrier beyond letter-writing, essays, the occasional article in an art magazine, and tackled a major project that, if successful, might just qualify me to add 'and writer' to my professional description. I had a manuscript novel on my hands.

The fifth circumstance, of course, was sheer luck. I submitted the finished thing to The Bodley Head, got a quick reading and acceptance. One or two revisions were suggested. Then in 1980 it was published. The odd thing was to have a pile of 30 'notices' — more notice taken of my single work of fiction than a lifetime of work as a sculptor. That took some swallowing.

That was the process, those were the circumstances. But that is mere process, the concatenation of events and feelings that started me writing and provided the opportunity to continue until an obsession was finally laid to rest, on paper. That is all the coat-hanger, so to speak. The clothes themselves come from a lifetime's experience, I suppose — not all of it, of course, but that strange, magical filtering process that I surmise distils into a poem, a novel or a play. The pattern of *doing* was already established in me as a sculptor.

So, the Quaker hero, the feelings about war, one or two of the characters perhaps, might be a bit of me, some my father (whose war had deeply affected me) and so on. My sculptor's habit of making art out of experience, without asking questions, but simply getting on with it even when the mind is blank, all this helped cross into this other medium. I had not realised how strong was this need to assuage the neglected Muse. 'Hell hath no fury' was the feeling implanted in me as the weeks and months went by and I dealt with political and administrative problems. I led this underlife of imagining, writing, imagining and writing, and revised and compiled like a miser sorting his lucre. The whole was a meeting of outer circumstances and inner necessity and a bit of luck. You cannot legislate for it. Had Paddy

McElroy not volunteered that excursion, had the obsession not taken me over, had I not received that nice little bursary from my poor belaboured staff, I might never have written beyond my usual compulsive sketchbook jottings and letters to my long-suffering friends.

It was a start. That was how I came to write. When the novel appeared under the title *A Tree May Fall* I was inordinately proud. I promised Bodley Head a sequel, I wrote it, probably too hastily and anxiously (I believe a fault with many first novelists trying to follow up an initial success), submitted it at once. It was refused. I revised it, and it was refused again. To compile, out of your imagination and experience, some 80,000 words, with characters, plot, geography and time all worked out, and then face refusal is such a love unrequited that words fail and it was time to take up hammer and chisel again — *and* to exercise a little humility, but to take heart.

When I was asked to give a year to Newcastle University, I found once again a verbal obsession taking hold of me. Having returned from Ireland to our wild peninsula, and now torn away again so soon, I found myself writing about that peninsula, as though it had never been settled, as though an old estate and its grand mansion had fallen into desuetude, and only a solitary, eccentric hermit lived in the burnt-out ruins of the old house. Otherwise no other soul disturbed the trees, the overgrown ivy, brambles and bracken that had taken over. Who was he? Where had he come from? Why did he require, or opt for, solitude? What did he do there? All this became another obsession, and my second novel, or rather my third, *Zorn*, came to be written. Now I knew the process. I lost my notes I'd compiled in Newcastle, found them the following year in Gregynog where another year of academic retreat followed. *Zorn* came forth and, on reflection, seems to me firmer, more economical, more rounded in style than *A Tree May Fall*.

The habit of writing thus extended beyond letter, sketchbook or the occasional essay for some magazine. It became a second arm, something in reserve when my arm finally got too weak for the hammer and chisel. That was not the motivation, but it could help in the years to come. But it depends. Circumstance and obsession must come together. The original catalyst cannot be coaxed falsely, but one must be ready. The obsession must take root of its own accord, then the chance too must arrive. That is why bursaries, fellowships, foundations, are so important for the self-employed artist. If he is any good, society is properly rewarded, since they actually produce art and any decent society cannot live without art — or can they? I don't know — but that Irish wallet came in handy at the time, enabled me to write where I might not have persisted.

Beyond all that, there is the openness to all impressions, and I suppose they come differently for different people. Even habit is part of it. For example, every day I first walk for three or four miles in all weathers, mainly along our peninsula, almost like an animal staking our the territorial imperative. It is not merely exercise — it is a contemplative morning watch, a daily prayer, even a state of ecstasy on occasion. (Have you ever watched, for a quarter of an hour, a winter sunrise over mountains?) In the middle of rough woodland there is a dogs' cemetery which I usually make the centrepoint of my walk. It is sheer habit and if I happen to sheer off in another direction the whippet usually lifts her ears in that questioning mode of hounds. I actually lifted the wording of one tombstone, to one 'Cloragh', and put it in *Zorn*. The invention of the context, the manipulation of words to convey the feeling of being there, *alone*, gives immense satisfaction, rather like, I imagine, Marianne Moore rounding off that famous poem about a snail and its principle:

in the absence of feet, "a method of conclusions";
"a knowledge of principles,"
in the curious phenomenon of your occipital horn.

But I think you know, otherwise we wouldn't be corresponding like this. Anyway, I do hope this answers your query, if only in part. You'll never get the lot from any artist, as you well know.

Fraternally yours,

Acknowledgements

My thanks are due to various people and public bodies or magazines for permission to reprint material or photographs: Gwasg Gomer; *Y Faner*; The BBC; Lady Wheldon for *Petites Soeurs* and *Huw Wheldon*; David Sherlock for *Maquette* and *Still Life with Table*; Cyngor Dosbarth Dwyfor for *Etifeddiaeth*; Mr & Mrs J. Black for *Bertrand Russell*; the National Library of Wales for *John Cowper Powys* and *Clough Williams-Ellis*; the Estate of David Jones and the Welsh Arts Council for *Cara Wallia Derelicta*; Messrs. Alinari of Florence for *The Ludovisi Throne*; the Contemporary Art Society of Wales for *Jacob and the Angel*; Cyngor Dosbarth Arfon for *Cilfach: Kate Roberts*; Ian Skidmore for *Better than One*; David Holmes for *Corris Man*.